How to Be A SUCCESSFUL LEADER

BY AUREN URIS

HOW TO BE A SUCCESSFUL LEADER gives you systematic, *practical* method for appraising ıd mastering the problems of leadership. : is a method that looks at leadership in ·rms of everyday use and that is so flexible . can be used by many different people nder many different circumstances.

Mr. Uris points out that the vital key to ·adership lies in three basic techniques — utocratic, democratic, and free-rein. All eaders use one or a combination of these ıethods, but, says Mr. Uris, the question s *when* to use *which* method. He then ınalyzes each method and shows you how o tailor it to your personal needs and to ·arious situations.

Since successful leadership depends largely ıpon how the leader understands himself, ıis group, and his goals, chapters are devoted to each of these considerations. These chapters are tools you can use to increase leadership effectiveness, for they show you how to understand and handle the group under your direction; how to avoid internal discord and sudden crises, delegate responsibility and blueprint leadership, solve problems easily and effectively, shape attitudes and build communications, schedule work, coordinate long- and short-range goals.

Case histories and personal stories of people who have proved their leadership ability pin theory firmly to fact. And throughout the book are many self-analysis and evaluation quizzes which help you apply the various techniques to your own personality and problems.

Extremely readable, HOW TO BE A SUCCESSFUL LEADER is outstanding in its field — bound to be of direct help to individuals who are now, or who hope to be, leaders, whether in business, community, or social life.

AUREN URIS is associated with the Research Institute of America, an advisor to business firms, and he daily comes into contact with the many varied problems of leadership. He is the author of IMPROVED FOREMANSHIP and WORKING WITH PEOPLE.

HOW TO BE A SUCCESSFUL LEADER

Books by Auren Uris

WORKING WITH PEOPLE

IMPROVED FOREMANSHIP

HOW TO BE A SUCCESSFUL LEADER

HOW TO BE

a Successful Leader

AUREN URIS

McGraw-Hill Book Company, Inc.

NEW YORK TORONTO LONDON

HOW TO BE A SUCCESSFUL LEADER

For information, address McGraw-Hill Book Company, 330 West 42d Street, New York 36, New York.

Library of Congress Catalog Card Number: 53–8019

Published by McGraw-Hill Book Company, Inc.

Printed in the United States of America

PREFACE

"If I could only . . ."

You've doubtless heard many a business leader or executive express a wish starting with that phrase. And the wind-up of the sentence often lays bare the very heart of a leadership problem:

". . . get the full cooperation of my people."

". . . create a more harmonious work atmosphere."

". . . increase the effectiveness of my group."

What obstacles prevent wishes like these from coming true?

The successful leader knows the answer to that question. For he—whether he operates in industry, finance, commerce, or civic affairs—is sensitive to the *potentialities of people*. He's aware of the forces which bring about—or interfere with—the efficiency of his followers.

He's familiar, further, with the complex emotional network that exists between himself and his group—and among the members of the group itself. And he knows, finally, that to handle his leadership problem satisfactorily, he must understand and deal with the people he directs, *both as individuals and as a group*.

Successful leadership requires mastery of the human elements of the leadership job. Whether you are in a leadership position now, or hope to be one day, the ideas and suggestions set forth here can provide the basic answers on which effective leadership depends.

You come in daily contact with the *need* for leadership. If you guide the activities of others, you're continually confronted by your people coming to you with questions, requests, problems of a dozen different sorts.

In your leadership, they seek—

—direction of their energies;

—work satisfaction;

—personal growth.

How well suited are your leadership methods to the needs of your people?

You also have *yourself* to please. You expect your leadership role, for example, to bring you—

—prestige;

—a sense of achievement;

—emotional satisfaction.

To what extent are your leadership practices satisfying your own needs?

The objective of this book is to help provide positive answers to these fundamental questions. The ideas and suggestions you'll find in the following pages, taken together, constitute a new and *practical* approach to leadership.

The contents of these chapters grew out of dissatisfaction with some widely accepted—but unrealistic—ideas. It was in the course of my present work at the Research Institute of America that the contradictions between current leadership theory and practice first came to my attention. And it was with the assistance of my colleagues at the Research Institute—one of the most distinguished research editorial groups in the country—that the unanswered questions and contradictions were largely resolved.

Some of the conclusions were published in a series of articles in *Factory Maintenance and Management* magazine. The interest generated by these articles was immediate and considerable. Many of the country's leading business organizations, companies large and small, in the merchandising, mail-order, automobile, and chemical fields, requested reprints or further information. Educational institutions did likewise. And so did many individuals who found, for the first time, practical answers to leadership problems they faced in their personal and business lives.

It is my hope that this book, with its more detailed suggestions for effective leadership, will provide the answers to many leadership problems that businessmen are seeking.

AUREN URIS

ACKNOWLEDGMENTS

To the men and women who, by their cooperation and criticism, their arguments and suggestions, their approval and disapproval, helped turn the mill in which ideas are ground:

Phyllis Brown, Vic Bumagin, Don Colen, Robert Dobbins, Peter Drucker, David A. Emery, Carmela Garofalo, Gloria Guarnotta, John Kostmayer, Aaron Levenstein, John W. Livingston, Jr., Fred Miller, M. J. Murphy, James D. Neville, William G. Shepherd, Hugh Smith, Harry Tapper, Harry Lee Waddell, Helen Willyoung.

And last, but first in my esteem and affections, my wife, Bette Uris.

CONTENTS

APPRAISING YOUR LEADERSHIP

1 : *Your Future as a Leader*

For twenty-two years, Patrick Kinsella pushed nickels through a New York subway change window. But one day—June 17, 1948, the time 9:36 A.M.—a crisis interrupted the work routine.

A passenger dashed up to break the news: a woman had gotten her foot pinned between a subway car and the platform on the level below.

Mr. Kinsella sprang into action. He ordered another employee to call the police emergency squad. Then he slammed his change window shut and dashed down the steps.

The scene was one of terror and chaos. Here and there in the crowd individuals tried to help. Two men supported the victim between them, trying to take her weight off the pinned leg.

BIRTH OF A LEADER

Mr. Kinsella took command. He shouted to the passengers to come out of the car which held the helpless figure. Then he had everybody line up alongside the car and place their hands against the unyielding steel side.

Voices protested that it was useless: nothing that heavy could be moved. When they were all in position, Mr. Kinsella shouted, "Push!"

Housewives, stenographers, businessmen, and businesswomen obeyed the command. Imperceptibly the car tilted. That was enough. Several people lifted the woman and her leg came free.

ODDS IN YOUR FAVOR

Patrick Kinsella's feat demonstrates some key aspects of leadership. It spells out—

► The *need* for leadership that a crisis creates. Not until the commanding voice of Mr. Kinsella imposed direction on the throng, could constructive action be taken.

► The ability of an individual, when the chips are down, to fill the leadership role successfully.

The heroic actions of Mr. Kinsella are not unique. In your own experience you doubtless have seen similar examples of intelligent, spontaneous leadership. What's more, the chances are that under the pressure of circumstances, you, too, *could and would* step in and take command.

But leadership rarely functions under such extreme crises. As a rule your decisions must be made deliberately, based on (a) a knowledge of people; (b) the tools of leadership which are available to you.

The demands of leadership made on us daily, on our jobs, socially, in community activities, need never find us unready. We can take encouragement from the words of the American poet Sam Walter Foss:

> And in the average man is curled
> The hero stuff that rules the world.

There is no question that the "average" man possesses the power of leadership. The higher above the average you are the less "uncurling" you have to do.

VERBAL TNT

You will find that leadership is a touchy subject. Talk shop, discuss the weather, fashions in clothing, any item front-paged in your local newspaper and the conversation will go along calmly enough. But talk about leadership and the pressures start to skyrocket. Just think back to the last election.

It's a symptom that reveals a healthy state of affairs: people feel involved in the subject of leadership because, for the most part, *they are.* The problems of leadership one way or the other come close to all of us.

Consider these examples:

Heartbreak house. A friend of my wife's is a beautiful, charming woman. She's a housewife, but her house is always a mess. She's had a succession of cleaning women; baby sitters and assorted help come and go. "I can't seem to get them to understand what I want done," she says. She's got a leadership problem. It frustrates her otherwise pleasant existence, is reflected in the atmosphere of her home.

Embittered millionaire. Mr. R. T. figures his income in the hundreds of thousands. His operations range from raw cotton and acetate flake to name-brand merchandise. That's a lot of territory even in the textile field. But Mr. T. has a leadership problem: "My associates don't respect me." It embitters every moment of his waking life.

Manager in the red. A plant manager has been struggling to increase the efficiency of his plant. Try as he can, month after month shows him operating at a loss. He can't seem to get the wholehearted cooperation of his people. He's got a leadership problem—and an ulcer.

YOU?

Parents—all of them—have problems of leadership to wrestle with day in, day out.

So do teachers.

And heads of community and civic organizations.

And officers of clubs and lodges.

And people in management, from supervisors up to the highest levels.

And so does everyone who now guides, or at some later time expects to guide, the activities of others.

OTHER SIDE OF THE COIN

"When the king has a bellyache, the people groan," states the old proverb. And it's true enough. One way or another, followers suffer the effects of leader's difficulties.

Consider, for example, the employees—cleaning women, the baby sitters—of the frustrated housewife. They undoubtedly had a rough time of it.

And how about the associates of our textile tycoon? Haven't *they* got a problem? What particular kind of hell do their jobs become, having to work under a leader they dislike?

Have you ever been inside a plant that's operating in the red? You can sense the tension and insecurity in the workers' movements, words, eyes.

LOOK TO TOMORROW

Certainly, in terms of individual needs—security, job satisfaction, and so on—good leadership is a primary factor.

But another reason emphasizes the growing importance of leadership in our time. It can be demonstrated simply:

Consider the great discoveries and inventions of previous ages. We have *individuals* to thank for them—Aristotle, da Vinci, Newton, Pasteur, Kepler.

But the development of atomic energy, for the most part, was the work of *teams of men and women,* working under skilled leaders.

And here's a recent headline—"Vaccine May Wipe Out Flu Next Year." That hope is based on the work of the World

Health Organization personnel. Scientists working in forty-four countries under the supervision of the WHO teamed up to develop a preventive vaccine.

More and more, progress in our age, whether it's toward a virus killer, or success of a department store or foundry, is the result of people working in groups.

And people qualified to lead these groups are scarce.

Just look at the community groups, which one after another give up the ghost, or limp along under half a head of steam.

Ask the civic-minded electorate of most towns, looking in vain for qualified candidates.

Ask employment agency people with high-paying executive jobs going begging for lack of qualified people.

TOWARD SUCCESSFUL LEADERSHIP

In every case where you find faulty leadership, you find progress retarded, achievement held back short of its proper goal. It takes a *systematized method* effectively to remove the stumbling blocks. And once grasped, the method lies like a ready tool in the hand of the capable leader. This *system of leadership* is the core of ideas around which these chapers are built.

Some of the ideas may be new. Others are as old as man's first gathering together in tribes under an individual ruler.

One point should be emphasized. There is nothing in these pages that presumes to say: "This is the only way the thing should be done. Forget anyone else's theory, and your own experience in the bargain."

By all means, draw on your past for guidance. Whether you have led people or followed the leadership of others, check ideas and suggestions against what you have yourself observed, your own judgment as to what will and won't work.

THE ACCOMPLISHED LEADER

Don't think of improvement in leadership as an intellectual process. It *is* mental—at the *outset*. But the ultimate goal is to develop attitudes and habits of leadership that automatically furnish the right decision and action at the right time.

Just think for a moment of the difference between an expert automobile driver and a beginner. The novice sits at the wheel perspiring freely and mentally working out each move he has to make. What the experienced driver does in a split second, without any conscious thought, the novice may take ten times as long to figure out.

The process of driving is altogether different for the two men. But the expert started exactly the same way as the beginner. Gradually, the moves and decisions which came with so much strain and effort became instantaneous responses. In the same way, the leadership methods described can become an automatic, natural part of your leadership behavior.

FLEXIBLE LEADERSHIP

At the heart of the method of leadership explained in this book is the quality of *flexibility*. No two people are alike. No two groups are alike. No two situations are alike.

The possible differences are explained, the *significance* of these differences spelled out. You are put in a position to suit the handling of a problem to the conditions involved.

Above all else, this book is about *you*. It's concerned with the problems you face in guiding the activity of others. The ideas and information you will find here have the sole aim of increasing *your natural leadership ability*. In a very real sense, these chapters are a set of tools you can use to maximize your present leadership effectiveness.

LEAD 'EM AND REAP

Good leadership will help advance your personal success. It *also* helps your subordinates, in terms of greater job satisfaction and accomplishment.

Regardless of your place in the business, educational, or social world, the better leader you are the more you will contribute to your company, your community, your country.

2 : *Test Your Leadership*

"Know thyself," said Plato. And he wasn't alone. That same idea, in one form or another, has been attributed to many great thinkers of the past.

It remained to the twentieth century, however, for this wisdom of the ages—apparently all ages—to come full blown. *Psychoanalysis* is the name it has acquired.

Self-knowledge, the mental healers tell us, can make the sick well. But knowing one's self is not only mental medicine. It is a great stimulator and clarifier. One flash of insight, one slight improvement in our self-knowledge, can make the difference between befuddlement and understanding, between failure and success in our undertakings.

Accordingly, the quizzes you will find in this chapter may be the paper knife that opens to self-inspection some uncut pages of your leadership potential.

But the tests serve two other purposes:

They provide a starting point for a process that's essentially personal. You yourself hold the key to your leadership future. It's what you feel and think and do that decides your achievement.

The quiz represents, in a large sense, a definition of the term *leadership*. Rather than use a dictionary meaning, or coin a meaning that only makes sense *after* you have read the pages ahead, the questions present the kinds of problems you actually come up against as a leader of people.

Question: "If I'm not in the mood to take the quiz right now, may I skip it, come back to it later?"

Answer: "Of course."

Question: "If I prefer, may I take the test piecemeal?"

Answer: "The results are just as useful, whether you go through the parts all at once, or over a period of time."

RATE YOURSELF

The tests offer an opportunity for self-rating. You have a chance to sit down with yourself and come up with a rule-of-thumb measure of the effectiveness of your present leadership methods and ideas.

Answer all questions as accurately as possible. The *franker your answers, the more meaningful your score.* Some answers may come easily. A few may put up a struggle. But whether your replies are off-the-cuff, or the result of intensive soul-searching, try to have each answer represent your best judgment.

The quiz is divided into several parts. Each measures a different aspect of leadership. You may check your score either after each part or on completing the series. In either case, you'll find the answers at the end of the last test section.

I. ARE YOU REASONABLY IMPARTIAL?

1. A member of your group tells you that your chief assistant constantly is on the lookout for ways to discredit you with your people and your superior. Would you—
   (a) get rid of the assistant? ☐
   (b) tell the informant to mind his own business? ☐
   (c) talk to the assistant to find out why? ☐
   (d) check the statement to see whether and to what extent it is true? ☐
2. Two people are available for advancement; there's only one opening. It's tough because they've both been on the

job the same length of time, there's not a hair's difference between them. One is a good friend of yours, the other just so-so. In making the final selection, would you—

(a) pick your friend? ☐
(b) choose the other man, to show you're being fair? ☐
(c) stage some kind of competition between them? ☐
(d) flip a coin? ☐

3. An error has been made. The man responsible has been both careless and stupid. You know it would do you a world of good to bawl the daylights out of him. Would you—

(a) go ahead and bawl? ☐
(b) keep your temper in check, to show yourself and your group you're capable of self-control? ☐
(c) smooth over the whole matter for the sake of harmony? ☐

4. Would you refuse a reasonable request for a privilege from a person you disliked, if you could do so without being thought unfair?

(a) Yes. ☐
(b) No. ☐

5. One of your subordinates has done an outstanding job. If you put in a good word for him, it means a promotion to another department. But his departure would leave a serious gap in your work group. Would you—

(a) hold on to him? ☐
(b) recommend him for promotion, and get along as well as you could? ☐
(c) stall off his promotion while training a replacement? ☐

6. You learned something about a colleague that's fairly shocking. He's living in sin, or plays the horses, or, at any rate, is guilty of some practice which is considered improper. As far as you can tell, his shortcomings are not

reflected in his work, at which he's extremely capable. Which of the following would most closely describe your reaction?

(a) "If I were his boss, I'd fire him on the spot." ☐
(b) "I ought to have a friendly talk, let him know that what he's doing, in the long run, may affect his job." ☐
(c) "I'm going to make it very clear by the way I treat him that I disapprove of his conduct." ☐

II. CAN YOU SOLVE THE MYSTERY OF PEOPLE?

1. Think of one of your superiors, past or present. Which statement best describes your view of him?
   (a) "I never could understand what made him tick." ☐
   (b) "I usually could figure out the reasons for his actions." ☐
   (c) "His behavior was so screwy, only a psychoanalyst could have known what he was up to most of the time." ☐
2. You've put yourself out to be friendly with a subordinate, since he's unpopular with his co-workers. His repayment is to go to your boss with an unfavorable story about you. Once you had got over being angry, in which direction would your thoughts run?
   (a) "That's the way it is. You do a man a good turn and he knifes you in the back." ☐
   (b) "Poor guy. He's so emotionally mixed up, he can't form a friendly relationship with anybody." ☐
   (c) "I'm going to figure out a way to send him down the drain, fast." ☐
3. One of your subordinates bends himself into a pretzel to be nice to you. Your reaction to his apple-polishing would be to—
   (a) tone it down, to save him from the resentment of others. ☐

(b) encourage it, to let your group see that you can take that kind of relationship without playing favorites. ☐
(c) let the subordinate see that he can have your friendly consideration without having to "buy" it. ☐

4. A new member of the group, a rather timid person, has caught on to the work and seems to like it. One day he comes to you and asks for a transfer to another department, any other department. Would your first thought be to—
(a) suspect that he wants a better-paying spot? ☐
(b) try to find out what's frightened him? ☐
(c) feel that he's just been putting on an act about liking the work? ☐

5. "Ever since that new punch press has been installed, Boss," an assistant tells you, "Ed Brown has been running it in a pretty careless way." Which one of the following possibilities would you *rule out?*
(a) Ed resents the new machine. ☐
(b) Your assistant is trying to get Ed off the machine. ☐
(c) Ed Brown is an accident-prone. ☐
(d) Your assistant is an alarmist. ☐

6. You've just been made head of your company. At the celebration dinner your colleagues give you, you notice one of the men seems to be soured on the whole affair. You know he had hopes of getting the top job himself. Would you—
(a) conclude that he was emotionally immature? ☐
(b) decide that he'd be a good man to watch, since he was bound to be disloyal? ☐
(c) try to help him get over his disgruntlement? ☐

III. CAN YOU ROLL WITH THE PUNCH?

1. You're a personnel manager for an aircraft plant. You find turnover for a particular riveting job is terrific be-

cause the operation has to be done in cramped quarters. Would you—

(a) hire midgets? ☐

(b) take up with the production department the possibility of changing methods to avoid the operation? ☐

(c) accept the high turnover as an unavoidable "cost of doing business"? ☐

2. You're the father of three sons, fourteen, twelve, and ten years of age. It's a standard part of summer outings to go hiking up a mountain trail. You have always led the way, but this year your oldest lad asks for permission to go first. Is your reaction—

(a) a wry feeling that "I'm getting old"? ☐

(b) one of pleasure at the boy's growing up? ☐

(c) "It's safer to continue the way we always have"? ☐

3. In an argument centered on the old saying that it's not wise to change bosses in midstream, would you—

(a) argue for the change? ☐

(b) argue against the change? ☐

(c) argue *against* argument, but *for* clear pro and con statements? ☐

4. Your company has a policy of a given punishment for a given rule violation—let's say, a month's suspension for smoking in a no-smoking area. A new employee and an old-timer break the rule for the first time. Would you want to—

(a) punish them both equally? ☐

(b) go easier on the old-timer, explaining to all concerned that his tenure warrants more consideration? ☐

(c) consider the old-timer's rule-breaking less excusable because he *is* an old-timer? ☐

5. You strike up a conversation with a pleasant, intelligent stranger in the park. After a while, he tells you he is an

experimental psychologist. And he has proof, he further informs you, that contrary to expert opinion, the ability of people to communicate by means of thought waves, through telepathy, is a definite fact. Would you—

(a) wonder whether he might have something of interest after all? ☐

(b) be annoyed that you'd wasted your time talking to a person who is clearly a nut? ☐

(c) realize that many of our most cherished ideas in the past have proved to be wrong? ☐

6. Answer the following questions as rapidly as you can:
How many ends does a pencil have? ——
Two pencils? ——
Two-and-a-half pencils? ——

IV. DO YOU KNOW THE ABC'S OF COMMUNICATING?

1. If you wanted to commend a member of your group for an outstanding performance, which of the following methods would you select to give him the biggest boost?

(a) Post a note of commendation on the bulletin board? ☐

(b) Praise him before an assembly of the entire group? ☐

(c) Praise him in a face-to-face talk? ☐

2. You walk around a corner too fast. Several of your assistants are engaged in matching pennies and it's past lunch time. You want to show disapproval without embarrassing them more than they already are. Would you—

(a) say excuse me, and retrace your steps? ☐

(b) tell them to save it for after hours? ☐

(c) tell them to break it up, lunch time is over? ☐

3. You're a sales manager. You want to win the backing of your salesmen for a new campaign. Which of the following methods would probably get best results?

(a) you describe the campaign in detail, tell them you expect every man to give it his wholehearted support? ☐

(b) let them help in planning the campaign? ☐
(c) tell them the top ten per cent will get salary increases, the bottom five will get fired? ☐

4. Generally, would you say it's easy to trace rumor back to its source?
(a) Yes. ☐
(b) No. ☐

5. You're in charge of a molding department. Primarily because of carelessness, the scrap rate is mounting steadily. You're trying to get the seriousness of the situation across to your pressmen. Do you think it would be most effective to—
(a) call them together and bawl the daylights out of them? ☐
(b) heap all the scrap in the center of the floor with a sign in the shape of a tombstone, showing the dollar value lost? ☐
(c) keep separate records for each pressman and discuss these with them individually? ☐

6. One of your people has gotten into legal difficulties. After six months in jail, he's about to return. There's controversy in your group, the usual discussion, some for the man, some against. To best smooth his reentry in the group, would you—
(a) make it clear you'd fire anyone who makes it unpleasant for him? ☐
(b) call the group together and ask for suggestions on ways and means of making him feel welcome? ☐
(c) make it your business to be the first to welcome him? ☐

V. CAN YOU HANDLE THE DYNAMITE OF PERSONAL POWER?

1. You take on a new assistant. He's capable, but you're pretty sure he thinks *you* aren't. One day you find he's by-passing you, taking up matters with your superior rather than with you. Would you—

(a) discuss the problem with your superior? ☐
(b) fire the man? ☐
(c) give him to understand that he's stepped out of line, and that you don't expect a repetition? ☐
(d) prove to him that by reason of your experience and accomplishment, you're fully capable of being his boss? ☐

2. One of your assistants comes to you with a petition which everyone in the group has signed. They want you to cancel a rule that provides a week's layoff for an unexcused absence. You've made the rule to show you're not kidding about cracking down on absenteeism.
   (a) Would you go along with the petition, since it reflects the majority view? ☐
   (b) Would you say you'd be glad to cancel the rule, just as soon as attendance improved? ☐
   (c) To save yourself future trouble, would you try to find out who started the petition, since they are ringleaders of a move to buck you? ☐

3. Your company—you're a division manager—inaugurates an unpopular policy. In announcing it to your people, would you—
   (a) show that you're aware of the policy's unpopularity, but suggest a trial period before any conclusion that it is undesirable? ☐
   (b) make it clear that you disapprove of the rule, too, in order to retain the good will of your group? ☐
   (c) say in effect, "That's the rule, men, and I'm going to enforce it as long as it's on the books." ☐

4. One of your group has a violent temper. In the course of an argument with a colleague, he picks up a letter opener and is barely restrained from using it as a weapon. Would you—
   (a) have a serious talk with him admonishing him against a repetition? ☐

(b) tell others in your group to stay away from him as much as possible? ☐
(c) fire him? ☐
(d) insist that he see a psychiatrist in order for you to have the psychiatrist's advice as to how best to handle the case? ☐

5. The fates have conspired to put you temporarily in charge of a group of three-year-olds. One little boy starts beating another. Would you restore order by—
(a) spanking the aggressive child? ☐
(b) making the aggressor play by himself? ☐
(c) telling the aggressor to stop because his victim didn't like it? ☐

6. Generally, is it best to keep your people on track, their efforts channeled constructively by—
(a) a firm hand? ☐
(b) putting them on their own? ☐
(c) getting them to function as a group which would share in planning and so on? ☐

YOUR SCORE

Give yourself ten points for each question answered correctly. Score each section separately, and figure your total for each. By comparing your scores for each section, you can spot both strong and weak points in your leadership thinking.

You can use the evaluation below as a rough measure of how you made out:

SCORE	RATING
50–60	Excellent
30–40	Fair
Below 30	Poor

Incidentally, note that the *leadership quality* being tested has been substituted for the quiz headings, for example: I. Are

You Reasonably Impartial, is designated as Objectivity, and so on.

THE ANSWERS

I. Objectivity. The first part of the quiz focuses on your ability to see things from a general rather than a personal, view. It measures your ability to make decisions without being unduly influenced by irrelevant factors.

1. (d) This is the only move which doesn't have you jumping to a possibly false solution.

2. (c) Ordinarily, a contest would be inadvisable. But of all four possibilities, it's the only one which helps you make a decision on the basis of the ability of the two people involved.

3. (a) There is such a thing as being *too* objective. Self-control, under the circumstances described, probably would be more harmful to both yourself and the culprit than a nice clean explosion.

4. (b)

5. (c) It's the least of the three evils.

6. (b) Both (a) and (c) are emotional rather than logical reactions.

II. Understanding People. The second section of the quiz measures your ability to comprehend the thoughts, emotions, and motivations of others.

1. (b) 2. (b)

3. (a) or (c) Either (a) or (c) would make sense. But the encouragement of apple-polishing indicated in (b) would be sure to kick back in the form of resentment toward both you and the overeager beaver.

4. (b) People who frighten easily can be moved to extreme, almost hysterical measures, should they feel threatened. (a) would be a legitimate second thought.

5. (d) Even if your assistant is an alarmist, you'd want to check on his statements.

6. (c) Of course (a) may be true, but don't think you can dismiss a human-relations problem merely by putting a label on it, psychologically sound though the label be.

III. Flexibility. Do you find you can change plans on short notice, switch your approach when necessary? The questions of the third section give you some idea of how adaptable you are.

1. (a) This was done successfully during World War II. Although (b) is not an unreasonable solution, it indicates a rigid approach—"I can't change. Let the others change their requirements."

2. (b)

3. (c)

4. (b) The ability to take all facts into account, and not to apply rules by the letter, is one of the important skills of leadership.

5. (a) or (c) Either answer shows awareness that we don't know everything, one of the attributes of a flexible mind.

6. It's the third answer that counts, and it should be 6. Half a pencil has as many ends as a whole one.

IV. Communications-mindedness. This section measures your grasp of methods of putting across ideas to others, both by your selection of words and media.

1. (b)

2. (b) or (c) Either one of these moves contains the right combination of disapproval and face-saving for them.

3. (b)

4. (b) Studies indicate that backtracking on a rumor usually ends up in a blind alley. Read *The Affairs of Dame Rumor* by David J. Jacobson, if you're interested in the subject.

5. (c) Face-to-face discussion would probably create aware-

ness of individual responsibility, a prerequisite for improvement.

6. (c) Nonverbal communication will often hit home when discussion would only bog down in argument. Or, looking at it from another angle, your welcome is likely to be persuasive; a meeting might prove embarrassing all around.

V. Use of Authority. Knowing when to crack down, when to ease up, when to get your group to back you up, is another major key to effective leadership.

1. (c) A case of this kind warrants one warning, anyway.

2. (b) 3. (a)

4. (a), (c), or (d) Any solution but (b) would make sense in this situation.

5. (c) It emphasizes the rights of others.

6. (a), (b), or (c) This is that most objectionable of things, a trick question. But you'll find the correctness of all three possibilities explained in the chapters ahead.

ROAD TO SUCCESS

Whether you scored high, low, or medium in the quiz is of no great consequence in itself. What *is* important is the picture of the leader in action, the leader faced by challenging problems, the handling of which decides his success or failure.

Glance back for a moment at the Answer section. Notice the headings of the various parts: Objectivity, Understanding of People, Flexibility, Communications-mindedness, Use of Authority. These are key elements that go into the business of leadership. Any of these can be acquired. If they are *already* yours, you can sharpen your ability to use them. The pages ahead show you how.

THE VITAL KEY

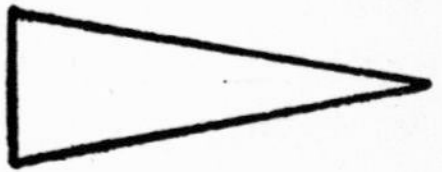

3 : *The Three Basic Methods of Leadership*

"The earth is flat."

"The moon is made of green cheese."

"Leaders are born, not made."

Whether you're talking about the earth's shape or the origin of leaders, false theory hampers progress and practice.

That's why, for example, as long as men believed in the "spontaneous generation" of disease agents, they were helpless to combat them. But when Louis Pasteur demonstrated the existence of bacteria, our fight against disease surged forward.

One by one, we've cast our false ideas about leadership. Unfortunately, many still remain. Here are two cases that show the kind of ideas hamstringing present-day practices:

CASE I

Superintendent Hal Byrnes is trying to break a production bottleneck in one of his departments.

"Tom," he says to his departmental foreman, "don't you think what we're up against is basically a storage problem?"

"Could be, Mr. Byrnes. Guess we are a little crowded. But we've got to have every one of these items close at hand."

"Think it over, see if there's anything you can do," requests Byrnes.

Week follows week. From time to time Tom gets a corner cleared, moves a lot of cartons from one spot to another. But the storage jam lingers on—and so does the bottleneck.

CASE II

Here is a second business executive's approach to the same problem:

"Jim, I've been checking your storage setup. It's got to the point where clutter is actually slowing down production. I want you to get moving on it right away. By tonight I want every aisle cleared. By tomorrow night I want benches free of everything but tools and work in process. And by the end of the week I want every bit of scrap sorted and moved over to salvage, where it belongs. I'll be down to check first thing Monday."

"O.K., Mr. Brown," says Jim.

Brown's orders are carried out. The result? An unquestionable improvement in the department's appearance. Definitely, an easier flow of materials. And, in a few days, a gradual rise in output.

BEHIND THE FRONT

If we could tune in on the thought waves of these two executives, we'd be likely to get something like this:

Hal Byrnes: "Maybe I didn't get results. But at least I handled Tom in the right way. I treated him like a human being. I gave him a chance to use his initiative and to participate in a decision that affected his department."

Mr. Brown: "I guess I got results," he admits, "but in the worst possible way. I had to put my foot down hard—right on Jim's neck. I know that's not the way to build a good working relationship."

Note this strange fact: Hal Byrnes *defends* his *failure*. Brown *apologizes* for his *success*.

Here are some widely accepted ideas about leadership that explain the views of men like Byrnes and Brown:

► It's not "right" to interfere in matters for which a subordinate is responsible. You take away his self-esteem.

► It's not "right" to issue flat orders. The right way is to "consult" and "discuss."

► It's not "right" to demand obedience from a subordinate. It destroys his initiative.

The two cases illustrate a major leadership dilemma:

The "right" way often fails to produce results. The "wrong" way is often successful.

HOW COME?

What accounts for this peculiar state of affairs?

The root of the difficulty springs largely from some misconceptions and misinterpretations arising from early experiments in the field of leadership.

In 1939, psychologists Kurt Lewin, Ronald Lippitt, and Ralph White, working at the University of Iowa, undertook to explore the nature of leadership.

Two sets of experimental groups were organized. One was dominated by a dictatorial leader, who

determined policy;

decided what was to be done and how it was to be done;

assigned tasks to individuals and decided the work companions for each member;

was personal in his praise, criticism, and comments in general.

The second group was led by a so-called "democratic" leader, who

brought up matters of policy for group discussion;

encouraged group members to participate in decisions;
permitted individuals to choose work companions;
was "objective" in his comments.

Then came an unplanned and unexpected development: one of the individuals playing the role of "democratic" leader was creating an atmosphere *different* from that achieved by other "democratic" leaders. He

exercised virtually no control over the group;

permitted group members to shift for themselves to a large extent;

had them tackle the problems that arose as best they could.

And the *group response to this technique differed* from the reactions of other democratic groups.

Lewin and his colleagues accordingly set up a third type of group to conform to this method, which they termed *laissez faire.*

RESULTS

Observers noted differences in atmosphere, behavior, feelings, and accomplishments among the three groups.

Dictator-led. Group members were quarrelsome and aggressive. Some individuals became completely dependent upon the leader. When the leader was absent, activity tended to stop altogether. Work progressed at only a fair rate.

"Democratic." The individuals got along with one another on a friendly basis. Relations with the leader were freer, more spontaneous. The work progressed smoothly, and continued *even when the leader was absent.*

Laissez faire. Work progressed haphazardly and at a slow rate. Although there was considerable activity, much of it was unproductive. Considerable time was lost in arguments and discussions between group members on a purely personal basis.

EVALUATING THE RESULTS

The imagination and keen thinking of the experimenters, the epoch-making nature of their studies, cannot be overestimated. Dr. Lewin and his associates made a major contribution to the study of group functioning.

But according to Dr. David Emery, an associate of Lewin's who conducted follow-up studies, many of the practical applications of Lewin's ideas have been misguided.

Take, for example, the very terms Lewin used. For purposes of his experiment, the words "autocratic," "democratic," and "*laissez faire*" were given specific and clear-cut meaning. But these words have general meanings and connotations. In many cases, these were substituted for Lewin's experimental definitions.

One result was the tendency to reject everything that smacked of autocratic and laissez-faire leadership.

For the term "autocratic," people supplied the connotations "dictator," "Hitler," "tough and unreasonable boss." For "*laissez faire*," the substitutions were "wishy-washy," "irresponsible," "spineless."

Another result was the overselling of "democratic" leadership. This was not the fault of "democratic" leadership. The error lay *in the misunderstanding of its method and limitations*. It is these misconceptions, about democratic methods, for example, that lead to the unrealistic situations typified by the Byrnes and Brown examples—a "hands off" policy with nothing accomplished, or intervention with feelings that "it's wrong to intervene."

CLEARING THE WAY

As has been said, the Lewin-Lippitt-White studies were eye openers. Distortion of the results in some quarters does not make less valid the fact that Lewin studies provide a sound starting point for an approach to leadership.

Actually, the three methods developed in the University of Iowa investigation provide an essential key. For the sake of clarity, let us define the three methods, under the names by which they'll be discussed in the following pages:

Autocratic leadership. The leader mainly seeks obedience from his group. He determines policy and considers decision-making a one-man operation—he being the man.

Democratic leadership. The leader draws ideas and suggestions from the group by discussion and consultation. Group members are encouraged to take part in setting policy. The leader's job is largely that of moderator.

Free-rein leadership. (Lewin's laissez-faire method)—The leader is more or less an information booth. He plays down his role in the group's activity. He's on hand mainly to provide materials and information. He exercises a minimum of control.

Much of our present difficulty lies in the fact that psychologists and sociologists haven't been content to *describe* these three different methods; they have also compared and *evaluated* them. And they have generally decided that democratic leadership is *best*. But the fact is:

► Autocratic leadership, *in certain situations*, will be effective and successful, when the democratic or free-rein approaches would fail.

► Democratic leadership, *under the right conditions*, will give better results than any other method.

► Free-rein leadership, also *under the right conditions*, will produce more successful results than either of the other methods. And this is true despite the fact that it is often written off as ineffective.

RECAP

It's worth repeating: the tools of the leader are the three basic methods—autocratic, democratic, and free-rein leadership. Contrary to common belief, these three approaches are *not* mutually exclusive.

No one has to choose between using autocratic, democratic, or free-rein methods, for example. That would be like telling a golf player he has to choose between using a driver and a putter. In the course of a game, he'll use *both.*

Note Mr. X, a successful plant manager:

► He *directs* his secretary to make up a report, on all overtime worked on a special order, until the order is completed.

► He *consults* with his five department heads on the best way to push a special order through their departments with a minimum of upset to regular production.

► He *suggests* to his assistant that it would be a good idea to figure out ways in which they can handle special orders a little more smoothly in the future.

Note the different approaches Mr. X is using. He orders (autocratic) on one phase of the problem; he consults (democratic method) on another phase; and he suggests an objective (free rein) in planning for similar problems.

The skill of leadership lies largely in knowing *when* to use *which* method. Your problem, then, is to learn to vary techniques to fit the changing *conditions* and *people* you meet in your work.

The skill with which you apply the three basic tools of leadership—autocratic, democratic, and free-rein techniques—determines your personal success as a leader.

The chapters ahead show you how to master this leadership skill in terms of specific problems, situations, and people.

4 : *More About the Methods*

A couple of young Italian farm hands were headed toward Naples for romance and adventure.

"If you get into trouble," cautioned Alberto, the more experienced of the two, "don't give your right name."

They met at an agreed-upon rendezvous when it was time to return home.

"Pietro," exclaimed Alberto, "what happened to you! The bandages, the blood!"

"I got into a little trouble with the police. They asked my name and I gave them a false one, as you suggested. And this is the result."

"How is that possible? What name did you give?"

"Benito Mussolini."

We can be fully aware of the importance of names, and still make a poor choice.

This is the case with the names of the three basic methods of leadership. The words "autocratic," "democratic," "free rein" are not the most desirable labels for the methods they signify. Still, they are used here because to change them to something else would cause even more confusion.

MEANING AND FEELING

As one semanticist puts it, "Words can make love and pick fights."

The process of twentieth-century education, for instance,

is likely to have given many of us an unfavorable reaction to the word *autocratic*. In the same way, few of us reach maturity without having strong pro feelings for the word *democratic*. Even the term *free rein* has its emotional weight. But here individual reactions are likely to differ.

You can learn your own reaction by a brief word-association test. Go down the following list of cue words, one at a time, as rapidly as possible. Write down or make a mental note of the word you associate with each:

CUE	RESPONSE
1. black (example)	bad
2. neat	____
3. industrious	____
4. speed boat	____
5. free rein	____

The first four words have no special significance. Their function is to establish the pattern of response. It's your answer to the term *free rein* that's important. People taking the test generally show one of two reactions:

Favorable. For one group, the term free rein draws such associated words as *freedom, liberty, independence.*

Unfavorable. For the opposed group, free rein has such connotations as *loose, aimless, no place to go.*

TOOL DESCRIPTIONS

Remember the last time you looked through a mail-order catalogue? Do you recall how carefully each item, be it an article of clothing or an incubator, was described? The mail-order houses long ago learned that, for best selling results, merchandise has to be described as completely and accurately as possible.

It will make for smoother sailing in the pages ahead if at the outset, the three terms, the three tools of leadership, are described as carefully as possible. It's advisable not only because the words have everyday meanings that may differ from those given in this book; in addition, the terms as used by Lewin and other investigators came to have meanings which differed from one another and, in some respects, from the meanings intended here.

Let's begin by getting a couple of loose pebbles out of the road. Here are some of the things the terms *don't* mean—popular notions to the contrary notwithstanding.

► Autocratic leadership does *not* mean dictatorship, or willful self-satisfaction of the leader at the expense of his followers.

► Democratic leadership does *not* mean putting all decisions to a vote.

► Free-rein leadership does *not* mean absence of leadership, a group left to lurch along without guidance or direction.

"CHECK SHOOTING IRONS HERE"

Let's try to do mentally what hosts of the Old West used to demand of their guests. Let's park our artillery—the preconceived ideas as to the meaning of these terms—at the door.

The fact is, it's important to shed any emotional associations you may have with the leadership terms in question. Your handling of these leadership tools is likely to be more expert if it is free of feelings irrelevant to the matters at hand.

Comparing the three methods shows that there are both similarities and differences. Note what they are in relation to some key points:

1. **Historical background.** It may seem illogical to say, on the one hand, that the concepts with which we're dealing are

unique and should be identified by new terms; and, on the other, to indicate that these concepts have histories which can be studied to good advantage. Actually there's no contradiction. No one quarrels with the anthropologist who seeks to understand more about modern man by studying the Neanderthal Man.

Two of the three concepts we're discussing do have roots in old ideas and practices. But the terms as we are going to use them do not coincide in meaning with their historical counterparts. Nevertheless, the basic ideas do have histories reaching back to antiquity. This background is of interest because it helps to some extent to explain present attitudes toward the terms.

Autocratic leadership, for example, is by far the oldest of the three concepts. Its origin and the first application of its methods were made by our half-brute prehistoric forebears.

Interestingly enough, in our individual history, the autocratic method is also the one we meet with first. The parent-child relationship, typified by the dependent child and the dominant parent, is one extreme form of the autocratic method.

The democratic idea has equally vague beginnings. But it was in ancient Greece that the term originated. And it was also in Greece that the governmental form described as "democratic" developed.

The free-rein approach, as a method of guiding the efforts of others, seems to have little historical precedent. Leaders of the past have undoubtedly used the method, but individual applications apparently never reached the stage of standardization, where the method was recognized as a usable approach to leadership.

2. **Relationships.** The main point of similarity among the three methods is that each can be used—under certain conditions—to guide the efforts of subordinates. They are not

extensions of one another; that is, they are not different degrees of the same thing.

3. **Centrality.** Each method focuses on a different element; that is, the energy and ideas which advance the cause of the group originate from different sources in each case. The differences can be represented in this way:

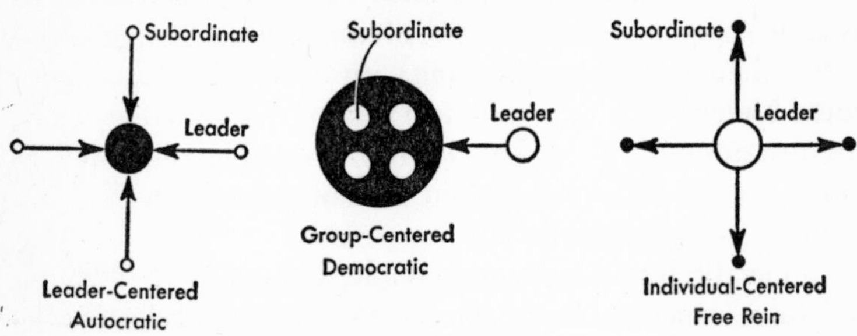

► In the autocratic method, the *leader* is the spark plug. His ideas, his plans are the ones that are carried out.

► In the democratic method, the *group* is the central element. The abilities, ideas, and energies of the entire group are a pool from which the leader gets the "materials" to build accomplishment.

► In the free-rein method, there is a multiple focus. Each individual in the group tends to become a supplier of ideas, and so on.

4. **Leader activity.** It is sometimes falsely assumed that an autocratic leader, for example, must be more active than a democratic one. Actually, the democratic leader may be as "busy" or even busier than an autocratic leader. But his activity is of a different *kind*. For the time spent by the autocratic leader in personal planning, the democratic one may be occupied in organizing a group of subordinates to do similar planning. And the free-rein leader may be equally active, again the difference being in kind, rather than amount, of activity.

5. **Responsibility.** There is no difference between the amount of responsibility shouldered by leaders using each of the three methods. In the final analysis, for example, each type of leader can fire a subordinate, or set in motion the purchase of necessary equipment, and so on.

6. **The moral angle.** It is sometimes thought that autocratic methods—and here the term "autocratic" is used in its general sense—is less desirable than democratic methods.

It is claimed, for example, that the individual under autocratic leadership is robbed of his natural dignity. Oppositely, the individual in a democratically led group is supposed to retain his individual dignity and self-importance.

These ideas frequently fail to pan out.

Under intelligent autocratic leadership, the rights of the individual may be *better* protected than under leadership which holds to the democratic method in form rather than spirit.

And observers have pointed out conditions under which the democratic method may become a tyranny. Where a majority rules, for example, the minority may constantly be suppressed and prevented from participating.

Nor is free-rein leadership necessarily a bed of roses. To some individuals, the free-rein method may represent a psychological ordeal to an extreme degree. The individual, for example, who needs close contact with his superior may actually suffer in a situation where he is put on his own. As a matter of fact, there have been cases where this "lack of contact" has been the method used to tip off a subordinate or employee to the fact that his presence is no longer desired. The discomfort of this isolation is supposed to—and often does—persuade him to quit.

7. **Effectiveness.** There is *no* difference in the effectiveness of each method. It cannot be said that the democratic method is *more* effective than the autocratic, or the autocratic *more*

effective than the free-rein. In a given situation you will find that each method has particular advantages and disadvantages.

SELECTING YOUR APPROACH

The next four chapters describe in detail the considerations you have to keep in mind to decide under what conditions each method is particularly suitable.

The four considerations—paralleled by the chapter headings—are:

► *the individual subordinate.* No two people are alike. The ways they differ, the effect the differences have on your method of dealing with them, are explained.

► *the group.* The make-up of your group exerts an influence on your method of handling it. The characteristics by which one group differs from another supply the key to your approach.

► *the leadership situation.* The life of a group has ups and downs, peaks and low points of activity and pressure. The extent to which leadership must change with the situation are clarified.

► *your own personality.* You yourself, the kind of person you are, often becomes the major factor in your methods of leading your people. Certain methods are better suited to certain personality types. The facts are provided which can help you make a decision along these lines.

At the outset, a basic question arises: does an approach that calls for a change of leadership method from one case to another, let us say, suffer from inconsistency? For example, how can you be an autocratic, democratic, and free-rein leader in turn, and not leave your subordinates completely up in the air? Doesn't such variation cause confusion?

The answer is a definite *no*—as long as the reasons for the change are understood by you. Consider the skipper of a sailing craft. He sets his sails and tightens his lines according to the prevailing winds and currents, changing them when necessary. He's not being inconsistent; he's being *flexible.* And it's the quality of flexibility—the suiting of leadership method to leadership needs—that is the supreme skill of the effective leader.

FROM DEATH TO LIFE

We face the same problem in leadership that the biologist faces. In order to study the vital organs, for example, the biologist frequently must separate them individually from the living organism. As soon as he takes this step, he is studying, not a living dynamic organism, but a dead one.

You must make the same mental reservations as the biologist. You must keep in mind that in analyzing these factors, one by one, we are actually pulling apart—and therefore changing the nature of—the process. Yet there is enough to be learned by this method to justify the move. The biologist's technique has given us our major advances in our knowledge of the life process. In the same way, our analysis of the suspended process can give us insight into leadership in action.

TAILORING THE TECHNIQUE TO YOUR NEEDS

5 : *Selecting Your Approach: The Individual*

I learned a lesson in leadership while sitting in a doctor's office on East Twentieth Street in New York City.

As I waited my turn in the crowded anteroom, through the thin walls of the apartment came the doctor's voice, shouting, "Stop worrying! Stop worrying, I tell you!"

I was shocked at the harsh tone where I would have expected sympathy and warmth. I heartily regretted the course of events that led me to that place and to that physician.

The consultation-room door opened, and the nurse beckoned me in. I entered and found myself face-to-face with the doctor.

He said pleasantly, "What can I do for you?"

During the next fifteen minutes he examined my ears and throat and gave me medication. His manner was friendly and considerate. I walked back into the waiting room, completely mystified.

The next patient, a woman with one child in her arms and another clinging to her skirt, entered the inner office. Immediately I heard—and couldn't help hearing, since the walls trembled at his full-throated roar—"I told you to stop putting that oil in her ear. Didn't I? Didn't I?"

A gray-haired old lady sat near the door to the outside hall. As I passed by, she said to me, "Isn't he wonderful?"

And then I realized that in many people a deep-seated need was satisfied by the scolding and noisy domineering.

Clearly, this specialist knew a great deal about his patients' psyches, as well as their bodies. The crowded condition of his waiting room testified to the fact that he applied his knowledge successfully.

YOUR SUBORDINATES AS INDIVIDUALS

In the everyday exercise of your leadership, you frequently deal with your group as separate individuals. Whether you're issuing orders or listening to complaints, you act on a face-to-face basis.

The correctness—more properly, the *appropriateness*—of the manner you use in these dealings will largely determine its fruitfulness.

As my experience in the doctor's office indicates, individuals have a preference for particular leadership approaches. The physician's extremely autocratic approach suited his regular patients fine. The democratic technique he used with me was undoubtedly an equally good choice.

I remember a second person I met with a natural understanding of the need to relate his manner to his subordinate's individuality. He was a foreman in a shirt-manufacturing plant in Pottsville, Pennsylvania.

"Jim can get along better with his people than any other foreman in the company," the plant manager told me. "And" he added, as though it were a contradiction, "he's had the least education."

After I had talked to Jim for a while, I asked him about his approach to his people. Could he explain it?

"Sure," he said. "I treat each girl different. If I want one girl to do something, I tell her. 'Damn it, Mae, shake your —— or you'll never get finished.' But use that same line on another girl and she'll slap your face. I just got a new girl. When I want her to buckle down to meet a deadline, all I've got to do is remind her. With her, it's, 'Margaret, will you please try to finish that lot you're working on as soon as possible?' You've got to treat some like ladies or they'll quit on you."

HOW TO JUDGE

How did Jim know *when* to use *which* approach? *Why* did the doctor adopt a *democratic* manner with me and an *autocratic* one with other patients?

You'll find there's scarcely a single characteristic of a person that *doesn't* influence your choice. Note some of these obvious points.

► *Age.* You'd tend to give a mature person *free rein* in a situation where a youngster would do best under the *autocratic* approach.

► *Sex.* Female chauvinists to the contrary, members of the pretty sex generally take to the *autocratic* approach, where, everything else being equal, the *democratic* or *free-rein* method would serve better with their brothers.

► *Background or experience.* The more familiar your subordinate is with his job or assignment, the more inclined you'll be to favor *democratic* or *free-rein* over autocratic leadership.

THE MAJOR FACTOR

But keying your approach to the individual depends in the greatest part *on his personality.* And here the recent work of social psychologists can be of direct help.

A group of psychologists—T. W. Adorno, Else Frenkel-Brunswik, D. J. Levinson, and R. N. Sanford—after years of theorizing, study, and research, were led to believe that there is a type of individual with a definite emotional predisposition toward autocratic-like leadership. They pooled their findings in a book entitled *The Authoritarian Personality.*

Here is a thumbnail description of the type, based on this unusual study.

THE "AUTHORITARIAN" PERSONALITY

His own town, country, language, he feels are best. He's provincial-minded, has a narrow outlook on most things. Economically and politically, he tends to be conservative. Conforming to customs and manners is very important to him. People who fail to conform are marked for his suspicion.

He dislikes "weakness"—either in individuals or groups. Therefore, minority groups draw his disapproval in greater or lesser degree. And by the same token, leadership which isn't "strong" is weak—and undesirable.

THE "EQUALITARIAN" PERSONALITY

Psychologists who have studied the concept of the authoritarian personality likewise speak of the "equalitarian" personality. It's possible to fill in the broad outlines of this type somewhat as follows:

He tends to be liberal-minded about most things—whether it's politics or the table manners his neighbor displays. Generally, he feels that people should be judged on individual merits, rather than on the basis of their religion, nationality, or the degree to which they conform to prevailing customs.

He doesn't like to be pushed around, doesn't like to see others pushed around, either. To him, therefore, the autocratic leader might seem to be "dictatorial"—and undesirable.

To him, democratic leadership and democratic processes—

such as discussion, majority rule, and so on—make emotional sense.

THE "LIBERTARIAN" PERSONALITY

Nowhere have I come across a description of a personality type which might correspond to the individual with the emotional predisposition for the free-rein approach. But it's possible to describe the type in general.

He tends to be somewhat of an introvert. He likes "to be on his own." He's self-confident, feels capable of working out means if he's told the ends.

Often he has a "technical" mind, and is likely to be highly skilled in his job. As a matter of fact, he tends to be attracted to activities, including ways of earning a livelihood, that require precision or an intellectual approach.

He's likely to think of direction from a superior as "control," and he's apt to confuse "control" with interference.

ADDING PERSPECTIVE

There's no doubt of the importance of the studies which have given us the concept of the "authoritarian" personality. But don't overlook the fact that these three "types" are not types of personalities in the full sense. They have as their central focus merely the response of people to leadership. Psychology is not yet at the stage where it can say just how these concepts fit in with more general theories of personality.

The findings and implication stemming from these studies broaden our insight into the follower-leader relationship. The concepts of the equalitarian and libertarian personalities likewise drive home the fact that individuals have a predisposition toward leadership methods.

AN ALTERNATIVE APPROACH

Of course, when you talk about personality, there's almost no limit to the theories you can choose from, each with its own terminology and "types." Some see personality determined by basic body types. Others found their system on the three basic emotions—love, rage, fear—and the extent to which each comes through in the individual's adjustments to his life situations.

Fortunately, you don't have to take a psychoanalyst's view of your people, or brush up on a comprehensive theory of personality in evaluating individuals. A rule-of-thumb method for sizing up your subordinates can give you the clues you need. Here, for example, are some personality types, as marked by *behavior*. Note the accompanying recommendations.

WITH THESE, BE AUTOCRATIC

► The hostile person. He resents authority. Yet his hostility must be met by a show of authority. The autocratic approach has the effect of channeling his aggressiveness, confining his energies to constructive ends.

► The dependent person. This type—typified by the patients in the specialist's waiting room—feels the need for firm rule. His sense of dependence gives him a feeling of being at loose ends, up in the air unless the leader is authoritative and dominant. Firm guidance gives him reassurance.

WITH THESE, BE DEMOCRATIC

► The cooperative person. Of course, the willingness to cooperate is not a distinct personality trait by itself. Yet when you find this quality in a subordinate, he will usually function best under the democratic method.

An individual who is cooperative is not necessarily unaggressive. But his aggressiveness, unlike that of hostile individuals, takes constructive paths. The cooperative-aggressive individual will head in the right direction with minimum control.

► The group-minded individual. The individual who enjoys "team play" will probably function best if your approach to him is democratic. He has less need for direction, since he regards his work essentially as a *group* job. He finds his greatest satisfaction in a friendly, closely knit group.

WITH THESE, USE THE FREE-REIN APPROACH

► The individualist, the solo player. He is usually most productive under the free-rein type of leadership if he knows his job. Even if he tends to be a show-off, a "grandstand player," let him have his head, unless considerations of *group* welfare, or resentments of other individuals give you cause to modify your approach.

► The social isolationist. Whether you call them introverts or describe them as "withdrawn," some people have an aversion to interpersonal contact. The actual reasons for such behavior, we are told, may be a latent hostility. In other cases it may represent a sort of low-grade schizophrenia, a lack of contact with the world of reality.

Whatever the cause may be, such individuals are likely to do their best work on their own. The atmosphere created by the free-rein approach is most conducive to their peace of mind, their most relaxed and effective effort.

WHAT KIND OF FOLLOWER ARE YOU?

You won't find it easy to arrive at judgments of your subordinates on which to base your leadership approach. People are complex. In the final analysis, they often defy the cleverest system of tags yet devised. Changes in the objective situation also can cause variations in both their attitudes and behavior.

But it is possible to gain a great deal of insight into this problem by considering *your own feelings* about leadership. Whether or not you now work under a superior, you probably have done so in the past. Analyzing your own feelings and reactions to leadership can give you the best possible approach to understanding your subordinates.

Answer the following questions, keeping in mind what you have done, or feel you actually would do, in the situations described.

	YES	NO
1. When given an assignment, do you like to have all the details spelled out?		
2. Do you think that, by and large, most bosses are bossier than they need be?		
3. Would you say that initiative is one of your stronger points?		
4. Do you feel a boss lowers himself by palling around with his subordinates?		
5. In general, would you prefer working with others to working alone?		
6. Would you say you prefer the pleasures of solitude (reading, listening to music) to the social pleasures of being with others (parties, get-togethers, etc.)?		
7. Do you tend to become strongly attached to the bosses you work under?		
8. Do you tend to offer a helping hand to the newcomers among your colleagues and fellow workers?		

YES NO

9. Do you enjoy using your own ideas and ingenuity to solve a work problem?
10. Do you prefer the kind of boss who knows all the answers, to one who, not infrequently, comes to you for help?
11. Do you feel it's O.K. for your boss to be friendlier with some members of the group than with others?
12. Do you like to assume full responsibility for assignments, rather than just do the work and leave the responsibility to your boss?
13. Do you feel that "mixed" groups—men working with women, for example—naturally tend to have more friction than unmixed ones?
14. If you learned your boss was having an affair with his secretary, would you respect him less?
15. Have you always felt that "he travels fastest who travels alone"?
16. Would you agree that a boss who couldn't win your loyalty shouldn't be boss?
17. Would you get upset by a fellow worker whose inability or ineptitude obstructs the work of your group?
18. Do you think "boss" is a dirty word?

To get your score, indicate the number of "yes" answers you had for the following questions:

I: 1, 4, 7, 10, 13, 16
II: 2, 5, 8, 11, 14, 17
III: 3, 6, 9, 12, 15, 18

ANALYZING YOUR SCORE

If you had most "yes" answers in Group I, chances are you prefer autocratic leadership.

If your total of "yes" answers was highest in Group II, you probably have a predisposition toward democratic leadership.

If Group III is the one in which you show the greatest number of "yes" answers, free-rein leadership is your preference.

If your score shows no preponderance of "yes" answers under *any* one of the three groups, the indication is that you're unusually flexible—so much so that you could adapt equally well to any type of leader. Another possibility is that your experience or predisposition is such as to make the role of follower more difficult for you than for most people.

Your experience with this quiz can be of considerable help in suiting your leadership to the emotional needs of your subordinates. Relate your score to your attitude toward authority, and you'll get some idea as to how *many of your people feel about you.*

6 : *Selecting Your Approach: The Group*

Group feelings and attitudes toward leadership were known to the ancients. Here's the way that early social psychologist and human relations expert, Aesop, tells it:

A colony of frogs, dissatisfied with their easygoing life, petitioned Jupiter for a king.

Jupiter, amused, tossed a log into the lake. Frightened by the mighty splash, the frogs fled in panic. But soon recovering, they approached the fallen monster cautiously. Since the hulk lay still, they moved closer, then swarmed over it, and finally treated it with the utmost contempt.

Dissatisfied with so tame a ruler, they again petitioned Jupiter, "Send us a king who will really rule over us."

Annoyed at their complaining, Jupiter sent down a stork, which promptly proceeded to gobble up the frogs right and left. After a few days, the survivors begged Jupiter to pity their plight.

"Tell them," Jupiter instructed Mercury, his heavenly messenger, "that it is their own doing. They wanted a king. Now they will have to make the best of it."

The attitudes of these frogs are human attitudes. And these group attitudes toward leadership have changed little, if at all, since Aesop's day.

GROUP ATTITUDES

Groups react to leadership in somewhat the same way individuals do. The group may feel "uncomfortable"—that is, dissatisfied—when leadership is weak or absent (King Log). It may become even more dissatisfied when leadership approaches the opposite extreme of tyranny (King Stork).

But before going into the considerations you must make in dealing with your group as a whole, an important question arises. And it's one that seems to run the leader into a dilemma. How is it possible for a group to be dealt with satisfactorily on a common basis?

In practical terms, the question can be put this way: let's assume you are the head of a group of fifteen people. When you deal with them individually, five of them do their best work under autocracy, five perform best when led by democratic means, five are most effective when the free-rein method is used. What justification do you have for giving preference to any *one* of the three methods when dealing with the group as a whole?

THE GROUP MOLD

Actually, experience and everyday observation tell you that groups can and do develop unity of behavior and attitude. What, then, of the individual whose requirements of leadership differ from the needs of the group as a whole? Is he carried along, despite his resistance, by the weight of superior numbers?

Strangely enough, these are *not* rhetorical questions. They are answerable to an extent.

First, let us face and grant the fact that many groups have their holdouts, unassimilated individuals who go along with the majority with varying degrees of unwillingness. Yet there are forces which operate in a group that tend to keep these to a minimum. What these forces are, exactly how they work, is only partially known. Just think, for example, of the gigantic task of describing adequately the melting-pot action of our own country.

Nevertheless, progress is being made. Studies of the interaction of people in groups are slowly pushing back the curtains of our ignorance. Some distant day we may know the whole story.

CAST FROM THE MOLD

Fortunately, a few milestones are already behind us. Here is a study which shows in part how leadership, group standards, and human interaction mold individuals to a group pattern.

Two psychologists—Herbert Fensterheim and Herbert G. Birch—made a study of a group of men and women in a DP camp in Italy in 1945–1946. Fensterheim and Birch noted that people in the camp tended to form into separate groups that differed in leadership.

Two of these groups drew their particular attention:

A. The "Militarists." This group was run by men who acted pretty much like officers in a military setup. They commanded implicit obedience. Their decisions were final. Emphasis was put on individual self-interest. For example, a member of this group who did outside work was permitted to keep the money he earned.

B. The "Democratic" Group. This unit was organized on a generally democratic basis. The leaders were elected and were entitled to no special privileges. Major decisions were made at meetings of the entire group membership. Leaders were responsible to the individuals who made up the group.

Group interest was stressed. Unlike the "militaristic" unit, for example, money earned by group members went into the group treasury.

DEVELOPMENT OF GROUP ATTITUDES

Dissimilarities were noted in the behavior of the individuals in each group.

Members of Group A were generally quarrelsome, aggressive, and tended to be emotionally unstable. Members of Group B were more emotionally stable, less aggressive, and as a group, more flexible and cooperative.

Unquestionably, the differing nature of the two groups attracted individuals who were predisposed to one or the other kind of group atmosphere. But—

The most important single fact that emerged from the study: *the behavior of individuals is affected by the character of the group to which they belong.*

FROM MANY, ONE

Joe Jones as an individual and Joe Jones as a member of a group can seem two entirely different people. Scientists explain this change by the concept of group forces that exists only when a number of people function together. Crowds in panic situations and lawless mobs are given as examples of these group forces at work.

You can check this idea yourself next time you're at a ball game or prize fight. Just watch the crowd yelling for blood: "Kill the umpire!" You can be sure that many, possibly those screaming the loudest, are ordinarily among the meekest and most mild of men and women.

A young schoolteacher with whom I discussed this phenomenon found an example in her own experience. She had taken a course in public speaking. In one of the sessions, designed to lessen self-consciousness, she had been asked to get up in front of the group and make passionate love to a chair.

"Ordinarily," she confessed, "I'm extremely proper. Why, I used to die a thousand deaths if I attracted attention to myself by sneezing in public. But that night everybody else was called on to do something extreme. And the fact that they were doing it--for example, a fifty-year-old dowager recited 'Mary Had a Little Lamb,' with gestures—made it seem all right for me to let myself go."

MORE MELTING POT

Out of the excitement, out of the rampant emotions of the group or crowd comes a ferment which acts on the individual like a magic potion. But mysterious though the results may seem, you don't have to accept them on an occult basis. Here again the psychologists have something to tell us. An experiment by Muzafer Sherif shows how group pressures affect individuals in their *power to observe* and in their *judgments.*

It's a fact that a small fixed point of light, flashed briefly in darkness, will seem to move. Different people see the apparent movement differently.

Sherif first asked a number of people, individually, to tell how far the light seemed to move. These judgments proved to be more or less consistent for each person.

Then the setup was changed. The same test was given to the same people, but now several took the test together. Each individual heard the responses given by others in the group. When called on to judge the movement under these conditions, *the judgments tended to converge.* The group responses were much closer to one another than the individual responses had been. *In effect, a group standard had been formed.*

Here's still another view of how the individual is changed by the group of which he is a member. Listen to this foreman's story.

"Last month the boss called a conference. I knew what it was about. It was to get us to work overtime, and believe me, I was dead set against it. I walked in intending to really let him have it between the eyes when he made the request.

"But when the subject was brought up, I was surprised to find most of the other fellows were perfectly willing to put in the extra hours. I was glad to keep my mouth shut, then. I guess I just had a cockeyed idea about the whole thing."

Note the rationalization he uses to explain his shift in viewpoint.

GROUP PERSONALITY

This conforming tendency that takes place in groups gives you the practical base to which to key your leadership approach. As a result of this unifying process, in which, of course, your leadership plays a part, you can consider the leadership needs of your group in the same way in which you weigh the requirements of individuals.

As a matter of fact, social scientists have given a name to the unity of attitude, behavior, and other characteristics displayed by groups. "Syntality" is the word they use, and they define it as meaning for a *group* what personality does for the *individual.*

It is with tacit scientific approval, then, that these phrases descriptive of groups find a place in our language and thinking:

> "They're a tough, hard-bitten lot."
>
> ". . . very cooperative."
>
> ". . . loyal, but they have to be shown."

JUDGING YOUR GROUP

Out of the countless pressures which bear on your people, specific group characteristics emerge. Your evaluation of these characteristics provides the keys you need in shaping your approach.

In suiting your leadership methods to the character of your group, you must take into account the attitudes, feelings, and background which hold for your group, and your group alone.

The problem you now face is this: how do you size up the character, or personality, or syntality of your group so as to know what leadership methods are most appropriate?

SIMPLIFYING THE QUESTION

Fortunately, the problem can be restated in more specific terms. Consider for a moment the labels that are sometimes used to characterize individuals. For example, a man can be said to be—

hostile
slow
unreliable
lazy
apathetic
willing
enthusiastic

These terms can also be used to describe *group* character. And so used, they are *not* figures of speech, but literal statements of fact.

The enthusiasm of a high-school ball team to beat its traditional rival is as real and characteristic as the enthusiasm of an individual scientist for a pet theory.

There is a similarity. *There is also a difference.* And because of this difference, we find ourselves stopped by a puzzle.

Let's take three of these characterizations which are most sharply defined: hostile, lazy, and enthusiastic.

As applied to groups, what is their actual meaning? What is a hostile group, or a lazy one?

Hostile—to what?

Lazy—with respect to what?

Enthusiastic—in regard to what?

These questions are important, because if they can be answered, we're well on our way to the answer of the larger question, of how to size up a group.

SYNTALITY VS. PERSONALITY

Compare the two concepts of individual personality and group personality.

We're pretty sure that the personality, or character structure of an individual is largely the result of childhood experience. Whether a man is to be a basically warm, out-going, cooperative person, or a hostile, withdrawn, and self-interested one, is determined in his bottle-and-diaper years.

But for the average group, there is no parallel. Groups grow and develop, yes. They acquire chronological age, as individuals do. They also acquire traditions, collective memories of their own past. But none of this adds up to the character growth of the individual. A group does not progress through a critical infancy which, for good or bad, leaves permanent marks on its behavior.

Then what is the *source* of group attitudes such as apathy, enthusiasm, cooperativeness? In the individual, these basic qualities result from patterns formed in early years. But how can we explain their source as group characteristics?

A specific case helps answer the question. Take as an example a typically hostile group—a group of employees that feels its legitimate grievances are unheeded. For the most part, its attitude will be unfriendly, uncooperative.

Now take that same collection of individuals and change the situation. Have them get together under their own leadership to discuss ways and means of solving their common problems.

Same group? Yes. But it's pretty clear that the spirit and attitude will be completely different. You're likely to find wholehearted cooperation, support for the leader, the same spirit you'd find in a Sunday-school group planning a picnic.

What's changed? *The principal change lies in the purpose or objectives of the group.* In the first case, the purpose, as they might have expressed it, was "to make a profit for those guys who won't give us a fair break." In the second instance, they were out to advance their own self-interest.

It would seem as though the *change in purpose* changed the character of the group.

USING THE CLUE

It becomes pretty clear that *group objectives, as contrasted to the self-interest of the group, will yield an important clue to group character and attitude.*

As a matter of fact, it's possible to phrase a single key question which gives us one of the answers we need in considering our approach to the group. It's this:

To what extent does the group work with you to achieve objectives? Let's go back again to the characterizations of hostility, laziness, enthusiasm. Now each term takes on a specific meaning.

A *hostile group* is one which either actively or passively opposes your efforts to achieve group goals.

A *lazy group* is one with insufficient motivation and lack of drive in assisting you to reach designated goals.

An *enthusiastic group* is one that shares your interest in achieving group goals.

ANALYZING THE QUESTION

Before you can answer the question, "To what extent does the group work with me to achieve group goals?" you have to consider—

1. How capable is your group of *understanding* group goals?
2. How *efficient* is the group's efforts toward the goals?
3. How *willing* is the group to strive for group goals?

Don't try to arrive at blanket answers. A great number of group qualities will influence these answers. Here are some of the factors to consider:

1. UNDERSTANDING

Comprehension? This is by no means a matter of I.Q. What's meant here is the general ability to grasp what's required.

Maturity? Not in terms of chronological age, but as indicated by such things as response to pressure. If your group's reaction to a request for effort above and beyond regular duty is adult—"It's got to be done, so let's do it"—then their rating in this respect is high.

Tradition? The length of time the group has been established provides another consideration. A new department, for example, in a rapidly expanding plant would tend to be less understanding of group goals. This might arise from the mere fact that the goals themselves have not yet been clearly established.

2. EFFICIENCY

Integration? How well does the group work together? How effectively do its sub-units tie in together? This represents somewhat the same quality for a group as does physical co-ordination for an individual. There is a wide range of possibilities, from the trained athlete whose every move is perfectly timed and waste-free, to the individual who trips over his own feet. The faster the *reflexes of your group*, the better it can concentrate energies and action.

Training? This factor covers both the amount of training and the *level* of training. The leader who views training as a continuing job will always get a better return for each man-hour worked. In general, the more *capable* your group is of doing its day-to-day work, the bigger its contribution toward reaching group objectives.

Experience? Another way of stating this factor would be, "How well do they know how to read your mind?" The more familiar they are with your own habits and approach to your work, the better they can anticipate your requests.

3. WILLINGNESS

Loyalty? This is the extent to which the group "sticks with you" and has feelings of personal responsibility toward you.

Cooperativeness? The group that will really put itself out to follow instructions, that will go to great lengths to work out problems you assign to them, has this quality to a great extent.

Discipline? The amount of authority you have to exert to keep them in line is an index of this factor.

DON'T USE ARITHMETIC

Don't try to gauge these factors in cut-and-dried terms. This is one case where it doesn't pay to look for numerical rating. Group character, like individual character, is too complex for that.

Suppose, for example, you supply point values to each factor and proceed to rate your group. You might get a "high" rating. But assume that the score has been based on very high ratings of Understanding and Efficiency factors, which offset low scores in Willingness factors. *Regardless* of how high you rate other factors, an unwilling group can't supply a positive answer to the key question, "To what extent does your group work with you to achieve group goals?" And weakness in either understanding or efficiency would likewise make an otherwise "high" score meaningless.

THE WHOLE PICTURE

You have to judge the answer on the basis of *all* the factors. And then you have to go one step further. You have to *weight* the factors. You have to decide which ones, for your group and for the purposes toward which group action is directed, are most important. As you will soon see, a single factor, absent or present to a great degree, may of itself determine your leadership approach.

DETERMINING YOUR METHOD

You may be able to arrive at a clear-cut evaluation. And you may not. After all, your group is subject to complex and shifting forces. Groups grow, develop, change. The addition of new people or the departure of old-timers all play a part in the change. Fortunately, it isn't necessary that you pick a label. For many effective leaders, evaluation takes the form of getting the "feel" of the group.

But at any rate, it's now possible to rough out an answer to the key question, "To what extent does my group work with me to achieve group goals?"

Note that a typical answer, based on an analysis of a group according to the factors which affect its character, cannot be given in one word. To be useful, the answer must be stated in terms like these:

► "My group works with me to the fullest possible extent, although hampered by its immaturity and lack of training."

► "My group works with me in a halfhearted way, and only strict discipline turns its efforts toward group objectives."

TURNING IT AROUND

Reversing the key question gives you the information you need to match your leadership methods to the character of the group. Here is one form in which the final question can be put:

"*What does your group need to get to help you achieve group goals?*"

In supplying the answer, think in terms of two things:

(a) Factors such as those listed on pages 62, 63 and 64—comprehension, integration, training, and so on.

(b) Methods of leadership which will best *strengthen weak points*, supply elements needed by the group.

Here are some examples:

A repair crew. In making emergency repairs, the major purpose for which the group exists, the biggest need is for speed and coordination. These factors are best supplied by the autocratic approach.

An average work group. Here you have most of the factors present to a normal degree. The lack is frequently in the means to make it possible for the group to contribute its total of experience, intelligence, ingenuity, and so on. The opportunities for participation provided by democratic leadership would probably yield best results.

A group of advertising copy writers. The principal need for such a group is likely to be mental stimulation, a seeking after the fresh and original. Personal contacts between group members and the leader, with the latter supplying both encouragement and high standards to discourage mediocrity of output, would be typical. These factors can probably be best furthered by the free-rein approach.

IMPROVING YOUR GROUP

Group personality isn't anchored as firmly to its past as is the individual. This fact points the way by which you can improve your group's contribution toward reaching group goals.

Take this case, for example, of a not unusual work group as described by its supervisor:

"I'm in charge of a polishing room. I've got fifteen employees, five men and ten women. They're on a pay incentive. They understand their work—polishing—perfectly. But they're interested in their own work and nothing else. Department quotas don't mean a thing to them. They look at every new job, and every new polishing material, machine, or method from one angle only: 'What's it going to do to my earnings?' They're a hard-bitten lot, and I feel that by now nothing can change them."

From the *short-range* view it's possible that autocratic leadership would be best for such a group. The immature, self-centered outlook of the group, the rigidity of attitude, suggest obstacles best handled by firmness.

But remember the concept that group character is *not* as firmly rooted as individual character.

From the *long-range* view it's possible that frequent use of democratic devices—group meetings, group consideration of departmental problems—might eventually build a group-mindedness which would help in getting group action toward group goals.

(Chapter 19 takes up the problem of short-range view vs. the long-range view in greater detail.)

7 : *Selecting Your Approach: The Situation*

In the heart of British Malaya lives a small tribe called the Senoi. According to Dr. Kilton Stewart, an English anthropologist who studied the Senoi for some time, the tribesmen are an unusually healthy, happy lot.

But it's from the viewpoint of its leadership that the tribe is particularly interesting.

In the ordinary course of everyday living, each individual does pretty much as he pleases. Yet the Senoi have no crime, no police force, and to all intents and purposes, *no active leadership* as represented by the usual tribal headman or ruler.

However, Dr. Stewart notes this change in the behavior of the tribe: when the Senoi face an emergency, people of authority do come to the forefront. When, for example, there is a threat of aggression from a neighboring tribe, elders of the community take over. The entire tribe then forms ranks under these leaders. A serious food shortage, requiring action by the tribe as a whole, also results in a change from latent to active leadership.

LEADERSHIP WEATHER

The situation in which a group operates always affects its leadership needs.

Where the situation is "normal"—whatever normalcy may

be for your group—other factors decide leadership methods. These other factors would be the personality of the group, your own personality, and so on.

But changes in the situation bring an additional variable to bear. Your awareness of this fact, coupled with suitable adjustments in approach, can help you over hurdles which might otherwise cause a major failure.

Changes in the situation in which you operate are apt to be frequent. In most work scenes, for example, there are always ups and downs—periods of greater or lesser pressure.

As a matter of fact, it is the element of *change* which largely creates the need for leadership. One way of looking at your leadership role is to consider yourself an *adaptation mechanism*, the means by which your group adjusts to the demands made upon it.

Governments considerably more complex than the Senois' understand this need to alter leadership to meet changing conditions. That is why, for example, the President of the United States is given war powers. As a more autocratic leader, he is better able to respond to the demands of the crisis confronting the nation.

TAKING STOCK

Keep in mind that a change in the "weather" or atmosphere in which your group functions doesn't *automatically* call for a change in your leadership method. This would be unnecessary, for instance, if your normal approach is suited to the demands which the change might require.

In addition, each leadership method is flexible of itself. You have sufficient leeway to handle most situations, both by your manner of using a given method and the variety of the techniques it offers.

But major shifts in the situation affecting your group do

call for a *reconsideration* of your methods. Here are some of the kinds of changes to which groups are subject, and revisions in approach which may be called for.

HANDLING INCREASED PRESSURE

It happens somewhere in the country several times a day—according to safety statistics.

A fire breaks out in an industrial plant. The department head, regardless of his usual leadership methods, is likely to handle the situation with words somewhat like this:

"Hank, close the fire doors! Bill, get the extinguisher! Ed, reel out the fire hose!"

Regardless of the department head's normal leadership method, an emergency such as the fire, calling for fast, decisive action, makes the autocratic approach a natural one.

There are other and less hectic examples of increased pressure on the group. More usual is the crisis precipitated by a rush order. There's a similar need for intensified effort, streamlined communications, and concentration of group activity.

There is a direct connection between degree of pressure in a situation and the feeling on the part of the group that it needs stronger guidance. In times of crisis people expect—even demand—strong leadership. When the pressure is off, the tendency flows in the opposite direction.

In a crisis situation, the approach that makes for effective leadership usually coincides with what the group feels is necessary. Generally the stress situation is best handled by autocratic leadership.

DEGREE OF CONTROL

The autocratic, democratic, and free-rein methods differ in the amount of control they exercise over the group.

This difference in the amount of control can be demonstrated visually:

The chart can provide a rule-of-thumb indication for revising leadership methods in response to increased pressure. Generally, the *more* pressure on the group—particularly when insecurity results—the *closer* to the autocratic area you may have to move.

It's an interesting fact that the chart contains useful implications for the leader who is ordinarily autocratic. Even in the army, for example, where leadership is generally of this kind, leadership in combat—the military version of intensified pressure—requires intensification of control even farther along the degree-of-control line.

An executive with whom this point was discussed, expressed the thought this way:

"When things tighten up, leadership must tighten up."

HANDLING INTERNAL DISCORD

The head of a small company once told me this incident:

"I have always been very close to my people. As much as possible I've tried to create a feeling of equality. We hold conferences to discuss company problems. Everyone gets a chance to contribute. And I have always prided myself on how well we all got along.

"Now I find myself in a tough spot, and I don't know what to do about it. Recently I had a disagreement with one of my assistants. The result was that the whole place divided into two groups, one favoring his viewpoint, the other mine.

"All at once I found myself stymied. My attempts to conduct my affairs as usual haven't worked out. I get no cooperation in our group meetings from the individuals who take his side. And I find that the previously friendly relations I have had with these same individuals have disappeared."

As the example indicates, the forces bringing about a change are not necessarily external ones. Changes within a group—as in the case of the factionalism described—can be of such a far-reaching nature as to affect group outlook.

The solution the company president finally worked out was based on a re-evaluation of needs created by the new situation.

He changed from his previous democratic approach to an autocratic one. He took a strong stand. He made his views clear, explained the basis for adopting these views, and as his final step, stated unequivocally that these views would be the ones adopted in the company.

Here are the three steps that guided his reconsideration. These same steps may be applied to more complex changes.

1. Decide whether or not your normal method is producing—or will produce—satisfactory results in relation to the problem at hand.

2. Try to anticipate the possible results of changed methods.

3. Compare and evaluate the results.

In the example above, the democratic approach was no longer effective in the atmosphere of ill will and mutual hostility dividing the group. Substitution of the autocratic method, in which the executive asserted his authority, held out promise for success.

TAKING THE STEPS

Unfortunately, these steps aren't as simple as they seem. Note the first one, for example. It's quite possible that perseverance in his democratic method eventually might have eased group divisions for the department head. But how would he know?

Frequently, you have to make a choice between (a) persisting in your method and hoping that time eventually will be on your side, or (b) taking steps 2 and 3 and deciding, on the basis of your knowledge of the group, the approach to which it's most likely to respond most satisfactorily.

HANDLING UNCERTAINTY

Occasionally, the nature of the change confronting your group is one where the ordinary everyday course of business is replaced by a situation of uncertain outcome.

This is the kind of problem the department head faces, for example, when his company is undergoing reorganization. Rumors fly, fears multiply, employees up and down the line look for reassurance.

This kind of situation is generally one where the personal relationships between the leader and the group members require change. In simplest form, it is demonstrated by the actions of one top executive during a reorganization. During the weeks when the fate of the company hung in the balance, he made it his business to mingle with his employees as much as possible.

Just as at Valley Forge, where the ordeal was weathered by the personal presence and the words of encouragement of General Washington, so too the mere presence of the leader can help the group withstand the anxieties that build up in times of uncertainty.

This personal contact frequently can offer more reassurance than all the high-sounding communiqués ever written.

EXPLAIN YOURSELF

Don't overlook the fact, however, that a change in your approach to your group can of itself be an upsetting factor unless you explain it.

For example, you want to avoid the situation where your people say: "He never acted like that before; things must really be in bad shape." Eliminating this reaction is largely a matter of explaining the reason for your change of approach wherever possible.

The three types of change outlined above by no means tell the whole story. Changes can vary a great deal both in degree and kind. The basic mechanisms by which you adjust, too, depend on the nature of the change and the degree to which it affects the group.

Although the examples given don't exhaust all the possibilities, the basic changes made in each of the examples represent major areas of your personal adjustment.

► In handling increased pressure, for example, the basic leadership element changed was *degree of control.*

► In the second instance, handling internal discord, the basic element involved in the leader's adjustment was his use of *authority.*

► In the case of handling uncertainty, the basic element was represented by the *personal relationship* between the leader and the members of his group.

These three elements of leadership represent major points in which your method can be adjusted to meet changes in leadership weather.

METHODS AND MANNER

Remember, however, that along with changes in method should go changes in manner, and vice versa.

For example, take this situation: executive Bill Smith, ordinarily an autocratic leader, finds himself up against a serious production obstacle. After developing and discarding three or four solutions, he finds he is stymied. However, he is pretty certain that by using the combined knowledge and abilities of his subordinates an answer to the problem can be worked out.

Bill can call his group together according to the democratic methods of discussion and conference, and put his group to work on the problem. But the group will function much more effectively in its new role if Bill employs along with his use of the democratic devices, the democratic manner which accords to his people the feeling of equality with the leader.

With the question of the personal touch goes the matter of your personality, the subject of the next chapter.

8 : *Selecting Your Approach: Your Own Personality*

"Recently, I started a new job. And from the first day I had trouble, trouble with the people under me. Usually, when a problem comes up, I like to think it over, and consult with my group before taking action.

"But I have the feeling that this practice has made my people respect me less. Compared to my predecessor, who was the hard-fisted driving type, I guess I seem weak and wishy-washy. I don't think I am. But at the same time, I don't see what I can do about this situation."

YOUR PROBLEM?

The dilemma expressed in these words lies at the heart of many an executive's leadership problem. Between the lines, the executive is saying, "I am a democratic-minded person, and naturally tend to lead my group by democratic methods. But my group prefers autocratic leadership. What can I do about it?"

The problem is not unique. On the contrary, *we all suffer from it to some degree.* Everyone has a "natural" leadership style; it may be autocratic, democratic, or free-rein. But the other considerations which influence our leadership behavior inevitably force us to water down, intensify, or completely alter our natural inclinations. We may be inclined, for example, to give our assistants free rein. But their inability to fill the role of free-rein follower makes it necessary to use autocratic methods in order to get the work done.

FROM ROOT TO BRANCH

The cause for these tendencies, the source of our "natural" leadership preferences, is to be found in our own personalities.

Psychologists generally agree that every aspect of our behavior—from the way we walk to the side we choose on issues of the day—is a manifestation of our personality. And, depending on our personalities, we will prefer certain leadership methods more than others.

But to *what extent* do our personalities dictate our leadership method? Can we "go against nature"? How, for instance, can the democratic-minded executive in the problem situation described make a better adjustment to the needs of his group?

LEADERSHIP AND PERSONALITY

Based on observations of leadership in action, these facts emerge:

► There is a type of leadership more natural to you than other types. In the long run, you'll do better with this approach than with another.

► Every leader must nevertheless use each of the three basic approaches *to some extent.*

► Your personal preference of leadership method is definitely one of the major factors influencing your normal approach. *But,* where other factors such as the nature of your group or the situation dictate, it is possible to adopt a method which is a satisfactory compromise of all factors taken together.

TESTING YOUR PERSONALITY

Are you naturally an autocratic, democratic, or free-rein leader?

You *may* be able to answer the question off the cuff. But the odds are stacked against you. Cervantes wasn't kidding when he styled this matter of knowing one's self as ". . . the most difficult lesson in the world."

Johnny Smith meets a girl at a party. She tells him, "When I first saw you, you looked so fierce and angry." But as far as Johnny knew, he merely felt lonely, out of things, and miserable. Self-knowledge and self-appraisal is made difficult for us by a mountain-sized blind spot.

And so it may be that, though we've been running a department or a company, we may actually not know our natural leadership tendencies. This blind spot can prevent us from utilizing the leadership methods most in tune with our emotional needs.

Knowing the kind of leader you tend to be may make only a small difference in your day-to-day leadership behavior. Other factors may outweigh the personality factor. On the other hand, the new insight this information yields may help explain past dilemmas, and equip you to deal with future problems on a much sounder basis.

Fortunately, it's possible to get a practical answer to the question of your natural leadership tendencies. The answer may not be as comprehensive or as accurate as you could gain through psychiatric consultation, but it can serve to clarify your leadership role in one of its most vital aspects.

WHAT TYPE OF LEADER ARE YOU?

The quiz below can reveal to you in approximate terms the type of leader you naturally tend to be.

Some of the questions you'll be able to answer offhand. A few may require careful thought. But answer all the questions, and answer them as honestly and accurately as possible. Where the question asked has no ready answer from your experience, indicate what you believe you *would* do in the situation described.

When you've completed the quiz, go on to the directions for scoring and the analysis that follow.

	YES	NO
1. Do you enjoy "running the show"?		
2. Generally, do you think it's worth the time and effort to explain the reasons for a decision or policy before putting it into effect?		
3. Do you prefer the administrative end of your leadership job—planning, paperwork, and so on—to supervising or working directly with your subordinates?		
4. A stranger comes into your department and you know he's the new employee hired by one of your assistants. On approaching him, would you first ask *his* name rather than introduce yourself?		
5. Do you keep your people up to date on developments affecting the group, as a matter of course?		
6. Do you find that in giving out assignments, you tend to state the goals, leave methods to your subordinates?		
7. Do you think that it's good common sense for a leader to keep aloof from his people, because in the long run familiarity breeds lessened respect?		

YES NO

8. Comes time to decide about a group outing. You've heard that the majority prefer to have it on Wednesday, but you're pretty sure Thursday would be better for all concerned. Would you put the question to a vote rather than make the decision yourself?
9. If you had your way, would you make running your group a push-button affair, with personal contacts and communications held to a minimum?
10. Do you find it fairly easy to fire someone?
11. Do you feel that the friendlier you are with your people, the better you'll be able to lead them?
12. After considerable time, you dope out the answer to a work problem. You pass along the solution to an assistant, who pokes it full of holes. Would you be annoyed that the problem is still unsolved, rather than become angry with the assistant?
13. Do you agree that one of the best ways to avoid problems of discipline is to provide adequate punishments for violations of rules?
14. Your way of handling a situation is being criticized. Would you try to sell your viewpoint to your group, rather than make it clear that, as boss, your decisions are final?
15. Do you generally leave it up to your subordinates to contact you, as far as informal day-to-day communications are concerned?
16. Do you feel that everyone in your group should have a certain amount of personal loyalty to you?

	YES	NO
17. Do you favor the practice of appointing committees to settle a problem rather than stepping in to decide on it yourself?		
18. Some experts say differences of opinion within a work group are healthy. Others feel that they indicate basic flaws in group unity. Do you agree with the first view?		

YOUR SCORE

To get your score, indicate the number of "yes" answers you had for the following groups:

I: 1, 4, 7, 10, 13, 16
II: 2, 5, 8, 11, 14, 17
III: 3, 6, 9, 12, 15, 18

If you had most "yes" answers in Group I, chances are you tend to be an autocratic leader.

If your total of "yes" answers was highest in Group II, you probably have a predisposition toward being a democratic leader.

If Group III is the one in which you show the greatest number of "yes" answers, you are probably inclined to be a free-rein leader.

EVALUATING THE RESULTS

Regardless of what score you made, don't think of it as either good or bad. For one thing, the test was not designed to grade you on a good-bad scale. But even more to the point: the condition itself, the degree to which a person tends toward one of the three basic leadership approaches, should not be thought of in terms of good or bad.

The test helps you establish a starting point for your thinking. It provides a base from which you can take a fresh look at your leadership practices, from the viewpoint of your own emotional needs.

Accordingly, your score is neither a judgment on your past performance nor an omen of the future. The fact, for example, that in the past you've generally operated as a democratic leader, while the test results indicate a leaning toward autocracy, doesn't mean you've been "wrong." Nor would this result mean it's desirable for you to switch to autocratic methods.

What the test can give you is food for thought, and subsequently a basis for making alterations in your leadership behavior.

Here are the points to consider:

1. **You and the test.** Keep in mind that no claims of scientific validity are made for the test. However, it has been given to a number of people, and constant effort has been made to improve it. Ambiguous questions have been discarded, "colored" wording has been minimized. Finally, test scores have been checked against the behavior and work history of the people who have submitted themselves to the quiz.

In its present form, it can be said that 90 per cent of the subjects have agreed that the results make sense to them.

As far as your own results are concerned, you yourself are in the best position to pass judgment.

One suggestion: don't check your test results against what you *think* of yourself. Measure them, rather, by recalling incidents from your own leadership experience.

If, for example, your score indicates a tendency toward autocratic leadership, doesn't that jibe with the fact that when the chips are down, you move in and take over your group with a firm hand?

Or let's say your score indicates a tendency toward democratic methods. The fact that you normally get your group together for discussion and planning purposes would tend to back up the accuracy of the results in your case.

Second suggestion: if you really feel the test has you pegged wrong, go through the questions again. You may find that second thought may suggest different answers.

2. **Remember the aspect of leadership now under consideration.** It's a good idea, at this point, to stop a moment to get our bearings. The test was designed to answer the question, "What type of leader are you?" Implicit in the question are the statements "all other things being equal" and "under 'normal' conditions." The point has already been made that when all other things are *not* equal—in a crisis, or when your group is confronted by a particular kind of problem—these special factors decide your choice of method.

3. **Importance of the personality factor.** Don't underestimate the significance of your personality in helping you develop your leadership role.

Some authorities feel that in the long run your effectiveness as a leader depends on your developing those techniques which coincide with your natural tendencies. Doubtless this view is true to a certain extent. But it's like the statement, "Man is wrong to walk upright since his skeleton and general body structures are better designed for locomotion on all fours."

Theoretical conclusions occasionally fail to make much practical sense. This apparently "logical" statement overlooks a vital fact. It's precisely *because* man walked upright that he freed his hands. And it is the freedom and development of his hands which made possible the creation of tools and the mastering of fire, the foundation stones of his supremacy.

In the same way, the reasoning that "So-and-so tends to be an autocratic person, therefore he should stick to autocratic methods" falls short of being either sound or realistic.

Sound leadership requires that we don't always do as we prefer. And we all have to some extent the flexibility which makes various techniques and approaches possible for us.

A useful view is that, when neither the nature of the group you're leading nor the situation confronting it demands otherwise, the requirements of your own personality should determine your leadership methods.

4. **Let your personality enhance your leadership.** A manager of a real-estate agency to whom I gave the leadership test was quite disturbed by his high autocracy score.

"But I've always prided myself on my democratic treatment of my employees," he protested. On checking his experience, however, he agreed that "when the chips were down" (you can substitute "when the veneer was off," that is, when he acted according to his natural impulses) he was autocratic.

His next reaction was to start thinking in terms of changing his personality. I believe what he had in mind was an act of will by which he would repress his autocratic reactions and substitute democratic ones.

If personalities could be altered this way, there'd be little need for psychiatrists. But my friend was in less danger of succeeding in personality regulation than he was in undertaking a totally unnecessary course of action. Further talk got him to accept the fact that autocracy was no less desirable than the democratic method.

In your own case, keep in mind that your success in leadership must be made not by brushing aside the personal characteristics you have, but rather by strengthening your leadership technique with full cognizance of your personal tendencies.

In other words, don't submerge your own tendencies unless other leadership factors so dictate. For the well-being of the group as a whole, it's probably more important for you to derive basic satisfactions through your connections with the group than it is for any other member.

5. **What your score means.** Let's return now to your own test results. Besides learning which type of leadership suits your personality best, other possibilities emerge.

In general, there are four possible types of scores. Each carries with it certain implications.

► *High scores.* Any category in which you scored from 4 to 6 "yes" answers is one toward which your inclinations are strong. Let's say, for instance, that your score read like this:

autocratic – 5
democratic – 3
free rein – 1

Your autocratic tendencies would tend to be quite pronounced.

► *Low scores.* Another possibility is that your score didn't go above three "yeses" in any of the categories. Here's a score of this kind:

autocratic – 1
democratic – 2
free rein – 3

Behind low scoring you're likely to find an individual without strong impulses toward any of the three types of leadership. It's likely, in addition, that he is ordinarily not self-assertive.

► *Balanced scores.* A particularly interesting type of score is one of this kind:

autocratic – 3
democratic – 3
free rein – 3

Evenly distributed scores generally reveal a personality sympathetic to all three methods.

People who make this kind of score have a well-proportioned personality. It's a desirable balance. Under ordinary circumstances, they will have less of a problem in attaining flexibility in their leadership.

Such a score, however, is not usual. The reason is that the autocratic and free-rein methods often require emotional outlooks which are directly opposed to one another. And such conflicting elements seldom are found within the personality of a single individual.

In most cases, balance is less perfect.

Let's say your scores were slightly off balance—3, 2, 1, for example. Your autocratic preference is there, all right, but it's not too pronounced. Chances are, people with scores of this kind would find little difficulty in functioning as democratic leaders.

► *Unbalanced scores.* A score that is high in one category, low in the other two, has some clear-cut implications. Take this possibility:

autocratic – 0
democratic – 6
free rein – 1

It's a safe bet that a person getting this kind of score has strong leanings toward democratic leadership. In addition, he has strong tendencies *away* from the other two types.

In a case of this kind, it's a very real possibility that personal needs are exercising an *undue* influence on leadership methods.

Go back to the quote which started this chapter. The man who wrote that might very well have gotten the score above. And the letter outlines in fairly clear terms the kind of trouble which may result.

Individuals with one-sided scores can lead the way in showing how to offset any undesirable effects of top-heavy leadership tendencies. The following recommendations suggest some possibilities.

6. **What to do about your score.** The leadership preference test you took in this chapter can provide insight into problems that grow out of a conflict between your natural inclinations and the other factors which influence your leadership methods.

Once again, let us go back to that quote at the beginning of the chapter. It would not be unreasonable to suppose this possible course of events:

The writer—let's call him Ed Brown—takes the test and scores 0, 5, 2. Ed then reads the interpretation of his score: marked democratic tendencies, some inclination toward free rein, but a complete lack of autocratic feeling. He can then state his leadership problem in simple terms: "I can see now that my trouble stems from the conflict between my group's preference for autocratic methods and mine for democratic ones."

His next question would be, "What can I do about it?"

Here are the things that can help you, as well as Ed Brown:

(a) First, be aware of your need to give your natural impulses the once-over before acting on them.

(b) Pay particular attention to the *way* you assert your authority. It's in this area, possibly, that your personal preferences may be exerting an unhealthy influence. When the situation might suggest the need for strong, autocratic measures, democratic or free-rein tendencies might stand in the way.

(c) Test yourself by this question: "Are my reactions suited to the situations which cause them?"

If you tend to be autocratic, for example, it's perfectly natural for you to have an autocratic first reaction to a situation.

You won't be able to change the feeling.

But you can change the action.

Let's say you've been stung by the insubordination—perhaps it's "independence"—of a subordinate. The last straw comes in the form of a dim view he takes of one of your decisions: "I don't think you were right to change our buying policy on that sheet stock."

Your impulse is to say, "Just run that Purchasing Department the way I tell you."

But with awareness of your tendency to overshoot on the autocratic side, you can hold back that impulse, weigh the facts of the case. Maybe he's got a point there, maybe he's right. At any rate, the mere fact that he argues the matter with you shows a certain amount of job interest.

Reconsideration doesn't have to mean capitulation. A perfectly reasonable—and *autocratic*—reply might be, "You may be right, Bill. But go ahead on my say-so. I'm assuming full responsibility for the outcome."

One final point: occasionally you need only modify your impulses, take some of the one-sided edge off decisions, plans, and so on. At other times it may be necessary for you to act directly in opposition to your personal desire.

That's the case of the leader who has to tell himself: "I don't like to fire Hank. I don't like to fire anybody. But he has it coming to him, and for the good of the group I'll just can him."

Easy? No. But no one has ever assumed leadership responsibility expecting it to be easy.

CAN YOU DO IT?

The steps described can help you adapt your leadership to the requirements of your own personality and, at the same time, to adjust to the pressures put on you by the other factors which influence your actions.

The benefits, however, won't come automatically. The more you examine your leadership problems, the more you think them over—and yes, the more you experiment with your methods—the more certain your progress will be.

This, then, is the general pattern of fitting your own personality into your leadership picture.

PERSONALITY ASPECTS OF LEADERSHIP

9: *The Trap of Personality*

Some wives may take a dim view of the paragraphs to come. So may some husbands. But the facts have been known—and the conditions have existed—since our distant forebears first got themselves involved in the bittersweet situation known as matrimony.

MOUTH OF A GIFT HORSE

Look down the street of a typical community on a sunny winter day. Walking down one side of the street you'll see Mrs. Jones, aware, and hoping that her neighbors are too, that she is wearing an attractive fur coat.

On the other side of the street, sporting both the same feelings and a similar coat, strolls Mrs. Smith.

Both coats are gifts of the ladies' respective husbands. But there is a major difference in the circumstances which produced the gifts. To assess that difference, let's go back to the thoughts of Mr. Jones and Mr. Smith the instant after the coats were presented:

MR. JONES: I'm sure glad I could afford it. Now she'll look the million-dollar gal she really is.

MR. SMITH: Now maybe she'll stop nagging me for a while.

STRENGTH OR WEAKNESS?

Frequently, you can't adequately judge an act without knowing the motivation. To a superficial observer, both Mrs.

Jones and Mrs. Smith would seem to have equally generous husbands. But the facts indicate otherwise.

The actions of a leader must be scrutinized in the same way before you can judge their aptness.

Take a case where a leader acts on the basis of the kind of person he is, where, in other words, his action springs from his personality. Those much-discussed gentlemen Mr. A and Mr. B can make the example concrete:

Mr. A blows his top, tells off a subordinate in the most heated terms. In this instance, the action is both logical and desirable.

Mr. B, on the other hand, doing likewise, is putting his foot in his mouth, his neck on the block.

The important point is this: the results are dissimilar, even though Mr. A and Mr. B were following the dictates of their personalities. Why does one man's personality lead him into a desirable act, while the other, performing the same act, becomes a *victim* of his personality?

In the previous chapter, it was pointed out that a leader's personality is a major factor on which to base his choice of leadership method. Is that suggestion always a good one to follow?

Actually, there *is* a hazard. Falling victim to this hazard may be completely unavoidable. But even worse than not avoiding the danger is to be unaware of it—*even after it's happened.* Here's what to watch for.

SPOTTING THE TRAP

It's all very well to say: If you tend to be an autocratic-minded person, run your group—as much as possible—along autocratic lines. If you are democratic-minded, ditto. If you are free-rein-minded, ditto.

But—an individual may be autocratic for the *wrong reasons.* That is, his personal motivation may not be "healthy." And the same may be true of the individual who in all honesty thinks he is democratic-minded, or free-rein-minded.

An examination into the ways personal motivation may actually trap you into a blind alley of leadership may help clear up serious leadership faults and difficulties.

TRIAL BY JURY

PROSECUTOR: Please identify yourself.

WITNESS: I'm an autocratic leader.

PROSECUTOR: Why autocratic?

WITNESS: I believe the autocratic method makes people produce best.

PROSECUTOR: Have you ever tried any other method?

WITNESS: No.

PROSECUTOR: Then how do you know?

WITNESS: I—er—ah—that is—

PROSECUTOR: You haven't really given the real reason, have you?

WITNESS: No, I guess not.

PROSECUTOR: Isn't it a fact that you use the autocratic method because you tend to be an autocratic person?

WITNESS: Right, that's right. I never thought of it just that way, but I see it clearly now. I'm really an autocratic-minded person. I like to run things my own way.

PROSECUTOR: Do you really?

WITNESS: Sure I do.

PROSECUTOR: I have a medical report in my hand. It states that you have an ulcerous condition. Is that true?

WITNESS: I'm afraid it is.

PROSECUTOR: Would you care to tell the court about the origin of this ailment?

WITNESS: It's occupational. Any executive can tell you. . . .

PROSECUTOR: But in your particular case . . . ?

WITNESS: Worry! That's the cause of it. Every minute of my

working life is spent worrying: someone's going to do something wrong. I didn't make the right decision. My superior is going to find fault with a policy I've inaugurated. My assistant won't be able to follow my instructions. I've got a million details to attend to and only one brain and two hands. How can I manage it? How? I can't, I can't, I can't . . .

PROSECUTOR: Smelling salts, bailiff.

REACHED A VERDICT?

As a member of the jury, you can draw several conclusions from this emotion-ridden scene:

(a) The witness is in a bad way.

(b) His method of leadership may be running his business, but it's ruining him. Note the emotional conflicts and actual burdens his use of the autocratic method heaps upon him.

(c) He thinks his leadership method grows naturally out of his personal make-up. Yet, it's plain that he's using the method probably *least* well suited to his personality.

How come?

Just compare these two sets of reasons behind two different individuals' choice of the autocratic method:

HEALTHY	UNHEALTHY
Well-founded self-confidence	Fear that subordinates will fall down on the job
Superior knowledge of operations	A certain amount of personal pleasure (in some cases, verging on the sadistic) in exerting dominance over others
The ability to shoulder responsibility easily	The feeling of prestige that comes from being the "big wheel"

There are other and shorter ways of describing the "bad" as opposed to the "good" reasons for using the autocratic method. Psychologists have pointed out that frequently the insecure person—as typified by our man on the witness stand—feels that only by complete control can he keep matters in hand. There is no need to point out, however, that it is the selfsame insecurity which leads to the kind of difficulties suffered by our man on the witness stand.

OTHER VOICES, OTHER DOOMS

Both the democratic and the free-rein methods similarly represent mantraps for certain personality failings. Here are the two contrasts in individuals using the democratic method:

HEALTHY	UNHEALTHY
The leader has a real respect for the capacities of his subordinates	The leader is hesitant to shoulder responsibilities and mistakenly thinks that by using democratic methods he is sharing—and thereby lessening—his responsibilities
He believes in the effectiveness of group thought and group action	He is reluctant to use authority—in disciplinary situations, for example—and therefore hopes to have the group remove this unpleasant job from his shoulders

DEACTIVATING THE TRAP

The problem that these facts pose can be stated in this way: what can the leader do whose choice of method is the result of a *personality weakness*—the sadistic individual, for example, who caters to his sadism by domineering his group?

The unself-confident individual who uses the democratic method in an attempt to sidestep responsibilities? The man who cannot make decisions and who uses the free-rein approach as a means of pushing the decision-making job onto the group members?

Actually, in cases of this kind there may be no solution—only an alleviation, or making the best of the situation. But two considerations offer themselves:

1. The man who finds that his leadership is being unduly influenced by personality weaknesses should take heart in the knowledge that he is not alone. To some degree all of us are handicapped by such failings. The thing that makes the difference is the degree to which the condition exists.

2. Where serious difficulties result from the leader's personality weaknesses, self-awareness can help.

Here the suggestion made in the previous chapter is particularly appropriate. Keep in mind that the personality difficulty generally shows up first as a *feeling or reaction*. The sadistic individual who uses the autocratic approach might find himself saying, "I'm going to really bear down on X for that mistake he made. I've got to set an example for the rest of the folks."

The fact that such a decision may be unjust could become clear to a leader *before he takes action*. And self-knowledge—the awareness that there is a tendency on his part to bear down harder than the situation warrants—would help the leader modify his action.

As one management expert puts it: "It's lucky for all of us that we're judged on the basis of our actions rather than our first thoughts."

Whether it's seconds or weeks, the time between our first reactions to a situation and the moment of final decision can represent a safety zone, a period for reconsidering and tempering judgments.

10 : *Leaders and Followers*

Elbert Hubbard used to tell this one about John D. Rockefeller:

In the course of sizing up a prospect for a job one day, John D. suddenly asked, "Are you a leader?"

The applicant, whose virtues ran to simplicity and honesty, answered after a moment's hesitation, "I can't really say. But I can tell you this: I'm a good follower."

The great man grinned and said, "I've got a raft of leaders out there already. I sure can use one good follower. You're hired."

Although John D. didn't indicate the fact, there is a connection between leadership and "followership." Knowing the nature of that relationship can be extremely important to you.

LEADING AND FOLLOWING

To see the tie-in, turn back to Chapters 5 and 8, just long enough to refresh your memory of the contents.

Chapter 5 features the quiz, "What Kind of Follower Are You?" Chapter 8's quiz is titled, "What Type of Leader Are You?" A comparison of the scores that were made by individuals who took both tests is shown in the chart on the following page.

	Followership Scores			Leadership Scores		
Name	Autocratic	Democratic	Free Rein	Autocratic	Democratic	Free Rein
John Doe	2	4	3	2	3	3
Joe Smith	3	6	4	1	2	2
Mr. X	2	4	1	2	4	1
Miss Y	3	6	5	0	4	3
Mr. Z	4	4	4	3	4	3
Total:	52	92	64	Total: 38	70	50

Here's how the totals compare when put on a graph together:

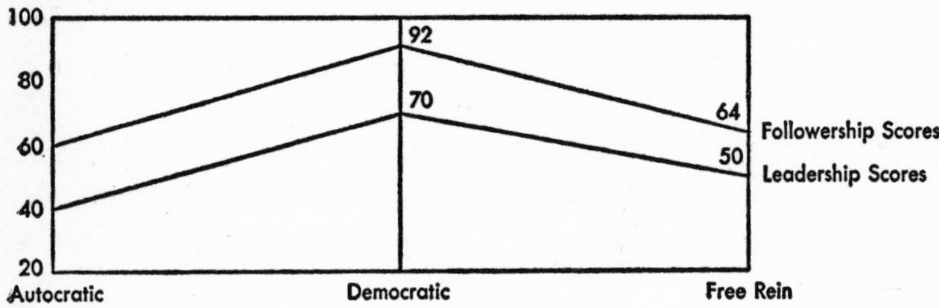

WHAT THE GRAPH SHOWS

The close parallel of the two lines shows a connection between the two test results. Here are some of the possible conclusions that can be drawn:

1. First, looking at the total scores of the two tests, it could be said—

(a) That in the group tested, the tendency toward democratic "followership" was pronounced. That is, the total score, autocratic—52, democratic—92, free rein—64, showed that as a group, the people tested showed a preference for *democratic* leadership.

(b) That the group's leadership tendency, as shown by the total score 38–70–50, *also* meant a leaning toward *democratic* methods.

2. Extremely interesting was the next possibility—that *people tend to prefer the same kind of leadership they would themselves give.*

Consider an individual case, that of Mr. X, whose score was 2–4–1 in both the followership and leadership tests. Although such close matching is unusual, it's typical of the *tendency*, as shown by group totals.

On the basis of his score, it's possible to say about Mr. X:

(a) In the role of follower, he prefers *democratic* leadership.

(b) In the role of leader, he prefers to use *democratic* methods in dealing with subordinates.

Of course, this same situation would pertain if the scores showed high ratings for the other two leadership approaches. Let's say Mr. Y's scores were, followership 5–2–2 and leadership 5–2–2. You could then say he prefers an autocratic leader and would himself tend to be one, if put in a leadership role.

PREDICTION VALUE

But the revelations of the graph become startling when you consider some of the less obvious implications.

3. *If you know the kind of a follower a person is, you can predict the kind of leader he will make, and vice versa.*

That's one strong indication behind the matching test scores. Here's what that adds up to in practical terms.

An individual who, as a subordinate, prefers autocratic

leadership will tend to use autocratic methods if put in a position of leadership.

CRACKING DOWN TO SMOOTH OUT

The experience of a works manager reinforces this point. The manager's assistant was a young man born and bred in the Pennsylvania mining country. Because of the mining background or other factors, young Tom exercised his authority over *his* subordinates with an autocratic hand.

The works manager, whose personal leanings were democratic, found his relationship with Tom most unsatisfactory. Nothing he could place his finger on, but he had the feeling that Tom's opinion of him, as man and boss, was mighty low.

One day a situation came up involving an inventory procedure. Tom's idea for handling the procedure differed from his superior's. The works manager, never one to be arbitrary, might have conceded the point. But he became aware that Tom was not so much arguing a point as trying to buck him.

The discussion was brought to an abrupt end. "Tom, we're going to do this my way, and that's final."

For the first time, the manager saw a gleam of respect in Tom's eye. He kept it there, he asserts, by keeping Tom on a short leash thereafter.

The point of the story is this: if the works manager had known the connection between followership and leadership he might have been more aware of Tom's followership needs, *since he knew the kind of leader Tom was.*

EXCEPTION TO THE RULE?

Contrary to the old adage, exceptions don't prove a rule. But frequently, *seeming* exceptions can provide a good deal of insight into the rule's limitations.

A case in point is the extreme one of the "nonfollower." He's the man who—

"doesn't want anyone to tell him what to do";
"doesn't like bosses in general";
"wants to be his own boss."

What's behind the make-up of this kind of individual? Usually, he's been given a tough time by his parents. His early associations with authority were unpleasant in the extreme. The result is that *any* kind of leadership—whether it's autocratic, democratic, or free rein—is viewed by him as repressive and restrictive.

People of this type often turn to the kind of work that will free them almost entirely from supervision. You'll find them in such occupations as mechanics, truck drivers—freewheelers of every kind.

But what happens to such people when put into leadership positions? If you can answer that question from your own firsthand observations, you'll discover the surprising fact that *even this seemingly exceptional case follows the rule.* The fact is, the typical nonfollower tends to end up as a nonleader. If given a leadership role to fill, he's apt to go off the deep end—at *either* end of the leadership range.

► He may become extremely autocratic, to the point where he is not autocratic at all, but dictatorial.

► Or he shrinks from the exercise of leadership altogether, adopts an extreme of the free-rein method that constitutes a complete lack of leadership.

But the fact that this seeming exception is not an exception doesn't mean the rule is infallible. Exceptions doubtless do exist. The chances are, however, that they exist on an individual basis. A person whose background or experience includes certain unique influences which tend to make him feel in a very special way about *either* followership or leadership might develop a different kind of followership from his leadership tendency, or vice versa.

THE IDEA IN ACTION

Very likely, in your own experience and observation you can find material that will back up the principles outlined. By and large, the value of an idea lies in what can be done with it. Here are some specific situations where the findings of this chapter may be of value.

BOSS TROUBLE?

Let's assume that you have a position of authority in an organization, but in turn you are responsible to a superior. Let's further assume—and it's not an unlikely assumption—that your relations with your superior are not as smooth as you'd like them to be.

One source of the trouble may come to light if you examine your relationship along these lines:

(a) Decide, either by the leadership quiz in Chapter 8 or by a combination of this test and a personal self-evaluation, on the kind of leadership role you prefer in relation to your subordinates.

(b) Then give some thought to your relationship with your superior. What degree of dependence—or independence—would be most satisfying to you? Would you prefer that he be autocratic, democratic, or free rein in dealing with you?

If, after these two considerations, you find that your relationship with *your boss* is decidedly dissimilar from the one you have developed with *your subordinates*, you may have put your finger on a basic sore spot of your boss trouble.

What to do from there depends on several factors. Let's assume that your superior is using an autocratic approach where a democratic one, allowing you more participation, would be preferable to you. In some situations, and with some types of individuals, you may be able to increase your participation merely by requesting it. In many superior-subordinate relationships, it would not be out of line for the subordinate to suggest:

"Why don't you let me handle that on my own, Mr. Smith? If I do have trouble, I'll let you know at once."

Whatever the nature of your attempts to make relations with your superior more satisfactory, remember that such a change must take place over a period of time.

CHOOSING AN ASSISTANT?

Let's say you are going to promote one of your subordinates to a position where for the first time he will exercise some degree of supervision and leadership over others. The question may arise as to which candidate among the possible choices will make the most satisfactory leader.

Checking these points for each candidate may help you arrive at a decision:

(a) What kind of follower is he? Your association with him can help you decide whether he prefers autocratic, democratic, or free-rein leadership in his role as subordinate.

(b) Knowing, then, what kind of follower he is, you can go on to predict the kind of leader he would make.

(c) The final step is to decide what kind of leader will be most effective with the people he will supervise, and to choose accordingly.

It isn't likely that you would want to make your selection on this basis alone. But in combination with other qualifications, and other factors which enter into making the choice, this is certainly one which can help you arrive at a sounder decision.

RECRUITING LEADERS?

This point applies if, for example, you're the head of a business, looking for people to run a company unit—department, division, and so on.

Directly at issue here is the dilemma that frequently crops up: should you promote from the ranks or select someone from outside?

Neither course is better, in all cases, than the other. But in making a choice, remember the basic principle that *a group tends to produce the kind of leaders it prefers.* Consider the test group which produced the scores used to form the chart on page 100. There's a strong likelihood that a man promoted from the ranks of this group will tend to be a democratic leader, since the followership rating of the group as a whole leans strongly in this direction. (This likelihood is actually borne out by the leadership-test results.)

THE UNTESTED GROUP

But now assume that you have an untested group. On the basis of your observations, you probably can decide whether the group tends to be autocratic, democratic, or free-rein in its followership. Having this knowledge, you are in a position to make a pretty good estimate of the type of leadership the group itself will furnish.

Let's say that under consideration is the leadership of a business office that has a tradition of autocratic leadership firmly ingrained. You can be pretty sure that the average rank-and-file member of such a group will tend to use autocratic methods, if put in charge.

In practice, the similarity of the leadership methods used by the man promoted from within and the methods preferred by the group *may or may not* be desirable.

If the performance of the group—and the word "performance" is used to mean all possible aspects, from output to morale—is fully satisfactory, then that fact is an argument *for* promoting from within. You have a pretty good guarantee that the leader you select will continue the methods that have proved successful in the past.

But if the performance of the group is *unsatisfactory*, the possible advantages of a change of leadership methods arise. A group, for example, whose achievement has been poor and that has a record of free-rein leadership may be up for a switch to autocratic methods. And such a change may be made more effectively by a man from the outside, who is capable of using autocratic methods.

CAN LEADERSHIP NEEDS BE CHANGED?

Don't get the wrong idea on one point. The above paragraph is not meant to imply that changing an entire group's leadership preference is a small task. Whole nations have been thrown into a turmoil of revolution in this very process.

Fortunately for many groups, however, such changes *can* be brought about without major difficulties. The problem of changing the leadership preferences of a group as a whole is taken up at greater length in connection with group goals, Chapter 19.

MORE POWER TO YOUR GROUP

11 : *Removing Mental Roadblocks*

The pistol-shot signaling the end of the game sounded, and its echo got lost in the roar of the crowd. The coach of the losing team headed disconsolately for the locker room.

One of the subs on the bench looked after the retreating figure and punched his helmet bitterly. "Too bad about the Old Man," he said. "He knows more about the game than anyone else in the business. But he can't do it all himself."

The player meant to be sympathetic. Actually, he was being critical. Because it's true of football coaches, foremen, company presidents, and any kind of leaders you can name—it's not what *they* know, but *what their "teams" can deliver* that makes for success.

FROM KNOWLEDGE TO POWER

That same idea can be stated more constructively: your knowledge of leadership must be transformed into the performance of your people in order to produce results. It's that knowledge, translated into greater capability of your people, that means a higher score on group targets.

Individual and group performance is an outgrowth of a number of group attributes which stem from your leadership practices. The next three chapters take up three especially important ones.

► *Attitudes*—the way your subordinates react to your leadership.

► *Communications*—the exchange of information, ideas, and feelings within the group, and between you and the group.

► *Personal efficiency*—the level of individual effectiveness of your subordinates.

In the chapters ahead, each of these keys to group performance will be examined at some length. But before getting into the practical details, let's make a preliminary over-all examination of the three factors.

MANAGEMENT THROUGH A TELESCOPE

An expert in the management field—where these terms have come up for special attention—would be quick to make two observations about attitudes, communications, individual efficiency.

First, he'd observe that the areas covered by each term tend to overlap. Attitudes, for example, are molded in part by the group's communications system. In turn, the quality of communications will definitely tend to reflect group attitudes. And as for individual efficiency, there's no question but that its level will rise or fall as attitudes and communications are good or bad.

Second, the management expert would be likely to tell you that the ground covered by attitudes, communications, and individual efficiency is vast. As a matter of fact, the three terms adequately blanket the entire field of everyday human relations.

Obviously, such a huge chunk of territory cannot be covered in a few pages. But in this chapter and the three which come after it, you can expect to find—

(a) a discussion of obstacles which *leaders create for themselves* in each area;

(b) a series of recommendations which tie your own activities to this important triple aspect of group life.

RESISTANCE TO CURE

Here's one of our country's outstanding business consultants talking:

"I've seldom gone into a top-level conference with company management without being told—

'We're all one big happy family';
'My door is always open';
'My business is different.'

"And I get these self-deluding statements even though the outfit may be in the worst possible kind of mess, organizationally and morale-wise!"

It's a fact that psychoanalysts remind us of: one of the biggest obstacles to therapy is the resistance of the patient. The phrases above are often the defense mechanisms which management hides behind to camouflage ineptness and inadequacy. Clearly, they stand in the way of even the preliminary examinations that can lead to diagnosis.

BEHIND THE RESISTANCE

Have you spotted the connection between each of the blue-sky statements and the three areas of group performance? They can be linked together like this:

Attitudes—"We're all one big happy family."

Communications—"My door is always open."

Individual Efficiency—"My business is different"—which is supposed to justify current levels of performance, or at least protect them from the hazard of comparison.

The question is: why do leaders of undoubted ability and unquestionable achievement kid themselves with these self-delusions?

It's an important question. And unless people in positions of leadership are willing to analyze their feelings along these lines, they'll be getting in their own way; efforts to do a job of building desirable attitudes, communications, and individual efficiency will be largely wasted.

THE "HAPPY-FAMILY" MYTH

To contradict the executive who tells you his staff is "one big happy family" would be, in many cases, as unkind as telling an ardent youngster there isn't any Santa Claus.

But there is a difference. There's no harm in the youngster's belief. But in the executive's case, his smug assurance may be the lid jammed on a pot building up explosive pressures.

This doesn't mean there are *no* "happy families." But in the life of most groups with an appointed leader, the attitudes of group members cannot be constructively viewed on a "sentimental" basis.

Loyalty to the leader? Certainly. But the essential relationship between you and your subordinates, to be practical, must be realistic.

A foreman I used to know had a gag that came closer to the truth than he realized. He'd pal around with his men off the job. They'd have lunch together at the neighborhood diner, frequent the local tavern for a few beers after work.

But as he and they entered the factory gate, he'd proclaim, "Now all friendship ceases."

Of course, it doesn't, in the full sense of the word. But the feelings between superior and subordinate can seldom remain the same on the job as in the off-the-job situation without causing trouble.

The trouble with the happy-family myth is that it tends to substitute a set of false values. It's the wishful thinking of paternalistic leadership.

The spirit in a group may be *similar* to that of a happy family. But the life of a business group, unlike that of a family, must frequently put emphasis on *achievement* rather than *contentment*.

QUESTIONS FOR THE HAPPY-FAMILY MAN

Let the executive who subscribes to the happy-family theory ask himself these questions:

"How *obediently* do his people respond to demands put to them?"

"How wholeheartedly do they *cooperate* with directives put to them?"

"When put on their own *initiative*, how successful are they in completing tasks?"

The questions not only strike at the heart of the happy-family myth; they also illustrate three basic responses—obedience, cooperation, initiative—your subordinates may have toward your leadership.

If the answers to the questions above can be given in a satisfactory affirmative, then the leader may indeed—and against all the odds—be correct in his happy-family assertions. If not, the contents of Chapter 12, "How to Shape Attitudes," is recommended for his consideration.

THE "OPEN-DOOR" MYTH

Resistance to taking a good hard look at the communications of a group is often summed up in that all-too-mortal phrase, "My door is always open."

I recently had the opportunity to confer with a top officer of a large banking institution. Our conversation eventually got around to communications within his organization. "Our communications are fine," he assured me. "I make it my business to reach almost all my people daily. I frequently stop by at their desks for a brief chat. And, of course, they know they're free to come in to see me at any time." (The open-door theme.)

"Do they come in?"

"That's the trouble, they don't. . . ."

And they don't for a good reason. The subordinate who *would* barge in on his boss—and it's this informal kind of contact that the open-door policy presumes—would be a most peculiar kind of fellow. He'd probably rate low in (a) tact, (b) a normal sense of values, and (c) regard for the wholeness of his hide.

Here again the feeling that "his door is open" is merely a sentimental substitute for concrete practicalities. The communications system of a group is as vital as the nervous system of the individual.

BIOLOGICAL COMMUNICATIONS

Consider for a moment what the nervous system does for the human being.

If his hand touches a flame, a signal is relayed to a motor command center that gets his fingers away before they are badly burned.

Take a more complicated situation. Consider the typical householder sweating it out over his monthly budget. Through his senses, his brain is given information by which he can allocate his funds.

His eyes inform him that his wife's wardrobe is in sad shape. And probably his ears assist him in getting this same information. He goes down to his basement. His nose tells him that the dampness is getting worse, and he'd better give more serious thought to a waterproofing job. On the way upstairs, his sense of touch tells him that his repair to the stairs was O.K. and will put him through another year.

THE GROUP'S "NERVOUS SYSTEM"

The communications system of a group, in somewhat the same way, keeps its leadership abreast of needs and developments.

Where the communications actually exist, this is how it works:

Lathe operator Ben Smith, working on a rush order, gets his hand caught in his machine. The nasty cut puts him out of action.

The department head has told his assistant about the importance of the rush order. Even though the department head is off the floor, the assistant gives the orders that will get Ben's machine back in the running, with a substitute operator at the controls.

On his return, the department head is told what has happened. He calls his superior and tells him of the mishap. "That means we'll have to ship a hundred pieces less." The customer can now be notified.

And Ben Smith? Good communications have helped him too. Thanks to the information given him by his boss, he knows where to go for emergency medical aid. He's resting comfortably in the doctor's office, recovering from shock and loss of blood.

COMMUNICATIONS OBJECTIVES

Communications in a group accomplish two things that are related but quite different.

(a) Communication unifies and integrates an organization. The left hand, knowing what the right hand is doing, can pitch in to help if necessary, or stay clear if that's desirable.

(b) Communication *contributes a sense of well-being* to a group. Above and beyond the fact that the group can respond better to various stimuli, is the "*feeling of knowing.*" It's this emotional by-product of communications that makes the difference between the man who feels secure and the anxiety-ridden individual in constant fear of the unknown and unexpected.

Opinion surveys have confirmed again and again one of the bitterest criticisms made of leadership: "We never know what's going on—we never know what's going to happen next."

Such doubts and fears make for friction, resentment, hatred, strikes.

IN PLACE OF A DOOR

Chapter 13, "How to Build Communications," takes up some of the communications systems available to you.

It's worth noting here that your method of communications tends to be affected by your leadership method. Actually, your communications system needs *change* with the nature of your leadership.

But in all cases, the objective is the same: the building of a positive and dependable system, rather than one left to chance in the form of an "open door."

THE "MY-BUSINESS-IS-DIFFERENT" MYTH

Of the three self-delusions, the last is likely to be the one uttered with strongest conviction. At least on the surface, it's the most impregnable. Obviously, every business is different from every other—in *some* respects.

Less obvious, but more to the point: every business is *like* every other in *many* respects. And usually, *the respects in which the similarities exist are the ones at issue.*

Actually, we're talking here not only of business organizations, but leader-led groups in general.

The head of one PTA group tells another: "It's only natural that your bunch is so much more active than ours. After all, our situation is altogether different. Our families are generally from the lower income brackets, their educational backgrounds are poorer," etc.

But none of the things mentioned explains why in one group the individuals are more willing to participate, undertake organizational tasks of one kind or another, while the other group drags along through a sea of apathy.

BEHIND THE EXCUSES

My friend the management consultant told me of this incident. He was asked to do a doctoring job on a large molding organization where productivity and individual efficiency were at marginal levels.

After a brief preliminary survey, he had a conference with the head of the firm and began to sketch out some of the possible remedies for the company's problems.

A lopsided wage scale was causing considerable dissatisfaction among the rank and file. The consultant mentioned some of the advantages of job evaluation, merit rating, and a generally new approach to rate setting.

"No good," said the company head. "That kind of stuff may be all right in some outfits. But our operation here is different. We're a job shop. Why, the plant even looks different one month to the next. . . ."

Behind most instances of the "my business (or group, or organization) is different" line is fear. It's a fear of the leader to face the evaluation of his efforts and success in terms of the performance of group members.

In the case of many businesses there's another angle. Consider for a moment the situation of the molding-firm president. Let's say that after a study by a group of experts, a new wage rate was set for his rank and file. And let's assume that the change meant a lower piece-work rate in many operations.

He's got a fight on his hands, from his people, from the union, from anyone who stands to suffer a tangible loss from the new setup. Certainly, the reaction from his people is understandable. But frequently the leader would prefer—and it's an emotional choice, not a logical one—to limp along down the road to ultimate disaster than stand before his own group and admit his failure to keep matters in line.

CAN INDIVIDUAL EFFICIENCY BE INCREASED?

The leader who accepts the fact that no matter how different his business is, his people can still be helped to perform at adequate levels, is free of a serious blind spot. He is in a position to both evaluate and improve the work of his subordinates.

In Chapter 14 you will find recommendations which can contribute both to individual and group achievement of desired goals.

12 : *How You Shape Attitudes*

A supervisor I know, called on to explain why a new employee had failed to make the grade, summed it up in two words:

"Lousy attitude."

But he didn't say *whose*—the employee's or his own.

Attitudes are the pace setters, the patternmakers of behavior, and can account for success as well as failure.

ATTITUDE FORMING

Attitudes can be headaches. If your subordinates don't have the "right" attitude, they will be handicapped in doing the kind of job you want. As a leader, you are in a position to develop the attitudes in your people that you feel are desirable, tone down the less desirable.

Trouble is, many people exercise their leadership in such a way as to *defeat* their objectives.

You see it in private life:

Housewife Jane Smith tells her cook, "Mr. Smith's boss is coming over for dinner tonight, Tillie. Prepare something really good, won't you?"

That evening Jane complains to her husband, "I don't know what I'm going to do about Tillie. That terrible mess she cooked up! I let her use her initiative, and look what happens."

And you see it on the job:

"Bob, did you schedule that XYZ Company order for next month?"

"Yes, Boss."

"But I see now we have enough material and machine capacity to have booked it sooner."

"But you told me to schedule it for next month."

"That's not showing much initiative, Bob."

Jane Smith and Bob's boss have made a common mistake. Jane Smith disapproves of her cook's choice of menus. Yet, Jane clearly *invited* the cook to use her own initiative (free-rein approach) even though she now regrets the consequences. The boss has been dealing with Bob on an *autocratic* basis. Yet he expects his subordinate to shown an attitude that *generally will never flourish* under that type of leadership.

Obedience; Cooperation; Initiative. At one time or another you find these three attitudes desirable.

But—

- ► how do you build them?
- ► how do you get the one you want *when you want it?*

Generally, you'll find this relationship:

LEADERSHIP METHOD	ATTITUDE OF SUBORDINATE
autocratic	obedience
democratic	cooperation
free rein	initiative

THE RESULTS YOU GET

Two facts are true about the twin lists above:

(a) If you use one of the leadership methods indicated at the left, you'll tend to get the attitude indicated opposite.

(b) If you want to *develop* one of the attitudes in the

right-hand column, the leadership approach indicated opposite is most likely to give it to you. For example:

If it's *obedience* you're after, your leadership should be *autocratic.*

If you want your people to be *cooperative,* that attitude will most strongly emerge through democratic leadership.

And if you want the initiative of your subordinates to increase, use the free-rein approach.

But remember, the leadership approach you use depends on the *kind of results you want.* None of the three attitudes—cooperation, obedience, initiative—is of itself necessarily more desirable than the other two. The situation you face at a given time will dictate your needs.

Let's say that you are under pressure to complete a job. The planning has been taken care of, the only problem is to get it done. At that point, any show of initiative on the part of your subordinates might gum up the works. The obedient acceptance and carrying out of your directives, on the other hand, could be expected to finish the job on schedule.

DEVELOPING THE ATTITUDE

In dealing with a particular subordinate or with your entire group, it's likely, then, that at different times you will want different attitudes or responses. This is both realistic and practical—if you are aware of which attitude you want at a given time, *and know how to go about getting it.*

The key to the attitude reaction you get—cooperation, obedience, initiative—lies mainly in the amount of *responsibility* you give subordinates.

With the *autocratic* method, you retain *full* responsibility for planning or policy setting. You say, for instance, "Hank, we've got a rush order from the ABC Company which requires sidetracking everything else in your department. Please start making the change-over at once."

Note, however, that you'd want to be pretty sure you knew just about as much as Hank does about the status of work in his department. You give him no leeway, for example, to suggest running a little longer, if that extra time leads him to a more convenient breakoff point. Using the autocratic approach in a case like this emphasizes that you want your directive followed *exactly as given.*

But install a control. Just make it clear you don't expect letter-perfect obedience when the consequences would be undesirable. You don't want to be like the office manager who insisted on having his orders "obeyed to the letter."

"Why didn't you tell me the building was on fire?" he demands of his clerk, after a harrowing last-minute exit down the fire escape.

"You told me you didn't want to be disturbed," comes the answer.

Using the *democratic* method, you *share* responsibility by including subordinates in the business of forming policy or planning. That comes about when you say, for instance, "Gentlemen, absenteeism is becoming a plant-wide problem. What ideas or suggestions do you have for dealing with it?"

Here you make the forming of policy a cooperative job. But just as with obedience, cooperation too may need a brake or control. There comes a point where you say, "Thanks for your ideas and recommendations. Thus-and-so seems to be our best course, and the one we'll follow from now on. . . ."

If you get individuals who want to continue to "cooperate" (prolong the discussion) after this point, you may have to emphasize that the decision has been made.

With the *free-rein* method, you put the major portion of responsibility on your subordinate. "Ed, we've got to finish that job by Monday. See what you can do."

In this situation, you've told your subordinate the goal, put him on his own as to ways and means of reaching it.

Needless to say, in all cases *ultimate* responsibility is still yours. A subordinate's share of responsibility exists only to the extent to which you've delegated—and *hold him responsible for*—the assignment.

THE BEANSTALK HAZARD

As has been pointed out, you want to avoid the consequences of attitudes carried to extremes. Uncontrolled initiative, for example, can be like Jack's beanstalk. Once it gets out of hand, there's no telling where it will end.

"But what in the world are we going to do with a million Number Six envelopes," wails the purchasing agent. "We only use twenty thousand a year."

"You told me to buy if the price was right," replies the clerk.

Of the three attitudes—obedience, cooperation, initiative—the last is the most volatile. Initiative on the part of your subordinates can be either your salvation or your undoing. Consider this case:

Air waves and front pages carried the story.

An unshaven "cowboy" walked into a swanky Vancouver hotel and asked for a room. The night clerk, deciding the man was an undesirable guest, informed him that no rooms were available.

As the cowboy climbed back into his car, a bellhop recognized him as America's number-one crooner, Bing Crosby. According to reports, the bellhop ushered Mr. Crosby back to the hotel and installed him in a suite.

Apparently the bellhop saved the day. But the question could be asked, *did the bellhop do the right thing?*

Just consider the position of the night clerk, for example. To bring the question closer home, let's say you make a decision about a matter, and a subordinate, acting on his own initiative, chooses to disregard that decision. *Even if his action turns out all right,* does he merit a medal or a bawling out?

CURING THE INITIATIVE HEADACHE

The general problem is: how can you give your people leeway without their going off the deep end?

It's an important point, because what *you* do about it will determine what your *people* do in future situations of this kind.

Three points passed along to employees encourage their initiative yet *leave you in control.*

1. **The information factor.** The bellhop knew something the night clerk didn't. His recognition of Bing Crosby underneath the crooner's "disguise" led him to act on his own initiative.

As an executive expresses it to his assistant, "If anything turns up to change the picture while I'm away, handle it according to your best judgment."

2. **The time element.** When your people are right on the scene, they shouldn't be expected to call the cook to pull the frying pan out of the fire.

To put across this idea you could say something along these lines: "Helen, that was a darned good try. I'm glad you made a stab at dealing with the situation, rather than letting it ride."

3. **Prompt notification.** It's doubly important that your people tell you the steps they've taken immediately after they've acted. First, it brings you up to date on a matter in which you have primary responsibility. Second, it gives you a chance to take follow-up action if the situation calls for it.

APPLYING THE STANDARD

Note how the keen-eyed bellhop fares by these standards.

1. **Information.** He recognized the crooner, which put him in the know, while the desk clerk was still unaware of the important fact.

2. **Time.** It would have been too late if he had reported *before* taking action. Therefore, an immediate move was called for.

3. **Notification.** It seems safe to assume that management was duly informed; otherwise there'd have been no news story.

Verdict?

Front! One medal, coming up.

SUMMARY

Keep in mind, then, that the degree to which you get obedience, cooperation, or initiative depends on the manner in which you tie down *responsibility.*

When you want obedience, *retain* full responsibility.

When you want cooperation, *share* responsibility.

When you want initiative, *delegate* the major share.

And spell out what you want when you want it. Your attitude requirements change with the situation. You're not being either arbitrary or unreasonable, for example, when you tell a subordinate:

"I know you usually make the decisions in these matters, Jack, but since this is critical, I'd better assume the entire responsibility."

You've made it clear you're switching the signals. He knows he's supposed to substitute obedience for initiative.

If you wanted to make the switch in the opposite direction, your words might be, "I'd like you to take over that problem and decide it—the way you think best."

And lastly, watch out for extremes of attitude which interfere with flexibility. *Too much* obedience ties your subordinates' hands. *Too much* cooperation can have your group actually overdoing a good thing. *Too much* initiative can take your train clear off the track.

Install the controls that keep you in touch with the situation.

TEST YOURSELF

By answering the questions in the following quiz, you can both analyze and evaluate your leadership practices. You can spot your weak points and strong points. In areas where you feel your leadership is under par, you'll find implicit in the questions possible methods of improving both your approach to leadership and the results you get.

Don't try to give the "best" answer. Give the one that seems natural or logical to you—what you would do if you faced the same problem. Keep in mind that this isn't a "psychological test." The scoring keys, which follow the questions, are arbitrary. They're included merely to stimulate thinking.

WHEN YOU USE THE AUTOCRATIC APPROACH

See how successful you'd be, as an autocratic leader, in forming the attitudes among group members that help produce results in an autocratically led group.

1. It's important for the autocratic leader to gain the obedience of his people. Would you do it by—
   (a) giving them the opportunity to discuss freely matters requiring decision?

(b) making it clear that obedience to orders is an essential part of job success?
(c) backing up directives or ultimatums by threats of punishment?

2. In your role of autocratic leader, it's important to win the loyalty of your people. Do you go about it by—
(a) accepting full responsibility for group actions, whether good or bad?
(b) maintaining a standard of personal behavior on a par with your people?
(c) sharing your leadership prerogatives with those who showed outstanding ability?

3. Would you maximize the desire for accomplishment by—
(a) telling your subordinates that ambition was the secret of your own success?
(b) generally accepting excuses for poor performance with understanding and sympathy?
(c) putting the group on a competitive basis with other similar groups? ("We've got to beat out the other departments," for example.)

4. Do you build group unity by—
(a) stressing the "elite" or special nature of the group? ("We're second to none in the company.")
(b) using group meetings or rallies for your "selling" sessions?
(c) forcing mutually hostile segments of your group to work together?

5. Do you stimulate personal satisfaction in the work by—
(a) direct personal praise for accomplishment?
(b) selecting a few individuals as personal cronies?
(c) stressing the material benefits which result?

6. Do you strengthen your leadership status by—
(a) picking as assistants those individuals having strong loyalty to you personally?
(b) insisting on constant activity by your people to pro-

hibit the kind of idleness that might breed insubordination?
(c) firing anyone you suspect is after your job?

7. Would you try to build loyalty to your organization or company by—
   (a) telling your people the organization is interested in their welfare?
   (b) emphasizing that it's a sound organization—been in business a long time, etc.?
   (c) emphasizing instances of interest in the individual's welfare—such as health and safety programs, retirement benefits, and so on?

ANSWERS

1. (b) As for the threats mentioned in (c): reprimands, yes; punishments, yes, but the autocratic leader who has to resort to threats and browbeating is slipping badly.

2. (a) The suggestion in (b) might work for a democratic leader, but the autocrat actually must put a certain distance between himself and subordinates. Thumbs should go down on (c) because, while the "trusted lieutenant" idea is all right, there should be only one boss.

3. (c)

4. (a) and (b) are *both* effective means of unifying a group.

5. (a) Tests have shown repeatedly that job satisfaction is an emotional factor, which doesn't correlate directly with material advantages such as salary.

6. (a) If you adopted (c), pretty soon no more subordinates.

7. (c)

WHEN YOU USE THE DEMOCRATIC APPROACH

See how successful a democratic leader you'd make, in so far as forming specific attitudes among group members is concerned. Keep in mind that these attitudes may or may not be desirable in themselves, but do help produce results in democratically led groups.

1. Would you foster team spirit by—
   (a) making clear the relationship of each man's job to the group goal?
   (b) razzing the "other" (competing) team, department, etc.?
   (c) stressing the fact that united effort is better than individual effort?
2. Do you keep individuals in line by—
   (a) threats of demotion, loss of privileges, and so on?
   (b) pointing out how their misdeeds are obstacles to group accomplishment?
   (c) getting rid of problem children?
3. Do you build cooperation by—
   (a) asking for it?
   (b) pointing out that those that don't cooperate don't stay in the group very long?
   (c) putting part of the responsibility on your subordinates by giving them a hand in planning?
4. Do you try to increase the individual's job satisfaction by—
   (a) encouraging friendships among group members in which you don't necessarily participate?
   (b) helping form small groups or cliques with which the individual can get a full sense of identification?
   (c) not letting him voice his grievances, on the basis that they'll eventually dissolve?
5. Do you strive to make your people respect one another by—
   (a) making it clear you believe no individual is more valuable than any other, as far as the group job is concerned?
   (b) treating them on a basis of equality in such matters as granting personal privileges?

(c) letting them get rid of their aggressions through some such means as approving the horseplay centering on a group "goat"?

6. If you were dealing with a subordinate who is low in self-confidence, would you try to improve it by—
   (a) increasing the importance of his assignments?
   (b) explaining to him that, on the basis of his job performance, his lack of self-confidence is baseless?
   (c) overlook his weak point, make the best of the situation within the framework of the man's acknowledged ability?

7. Your superior tells you of a policy announcement that is to be made that you know will be unfavorably received by the group. You let your superior know that a couple of previous incidents have already set the group on edge, and he suggests that it might be better if the announcement is made by him rather than by you, as originally intended. Would you—
   (a) go along with your boss's suggestion?
   (b) make the announcement yourself?
   (c) suggest to your boss that the announcement be deferred as long as possible?

ANSWERS

1. (a)

2. (b) You'd consider (c) only where the out-of-line activity borders on the irrational.

3. (c) (a) is a possibility, but not advisable from the long view. You can't eliminate the causes for lack of cooperation that easily.

4. (a)

5. (b) So far as (a) is concerned, the idea of equality extends to rights and privileges, not to comparative abilities.

6. (b) and (c) would both be effective, your choice depending on the individual with whom you were dealing. If you're a gambler, you might try (a). But you'd have to go slowly to avoid putting your man out on a limb.

7. (c), certainly. But as between (a) and (b), don't overlook this possibility: if your group is limping along, handicapped by a sour outlook, the strongest move you could make might be to precipitate a crisis which would bring all the pent-up feelings to the surface. Just be sure they're not strong enough to blow the place apart.

WHEN YOU USE THE FREE-REIN APPROACH

Now test your success as a free-rein leader in dealing with attitudes of group members. As an example of the situation in general, to give yourself a frame of reference, assume you're a leader in charge of a group of research chemists or other such highly trained people.

1. Do you build goal-mindedness by—
   (a) emphasizing how much successful completion of the task means to you?
   (b) keeping up a steady pressure for results?
   (c) standing at the finish line with a medal?
2. In your relations with group members, do you—
   (a) let them know they can fall back on you for support when they're stymied?
   (b) try to work with them as closely as your time allows?
   (c) try to keep personal relations on a neutral rather than friendly basis?
   (d) make it a policy that, in differences of opinion, your word is always final?
3. To foster desirable interpersonal relations among subordinates, do you—
   (a) jump right in with your doctor's kit in cases of frictions or feuds that interfere with the work?

(b) try to prevent personal ties among the group that tend to compartmentalize it, divide it into subgroups?
(c) keep up a constant but unobtrusive campaign to sell each man's virtues to his associates?

4. Do you maximize effectiveness of group members by—
(a) pep talks that center on the accomplishments of the outstanding individuals?
(b) removing the factors that distract effort from main goals, such as the hauling of materials and supplies?
(c) insisting that the poorer performers keep up with the top-notch people?

5. One of your top-notch people is responding to the lure of another job. Would you—
(a) tell him how much better your organization is as an employer, compared to the rival outfit?
(b) try to figure out what there is about his job that interferes with his job satisfaction?
(c) simply let him go?

6. A subordinate who you feel should be doing better, offers as an explanation of poor job performance the fact that he "isn't getting enough guidance" in his work. Would you—
(a) explain that, as a trained professional, he should be capable of getting along on his own?
(b) refer him to a psychiatrist, since he is obviously overdependent on authority?
(c) switch to either the democratic or autocratic method of leadership in his case?

7. You come into the room just in time to overhear two of your subordinates plotting a practical joke on a third. Would you—
(a) encourage it?
(b) discourage it?
(c) rage at it?

ANSWERS

1. (c)

2. (a) Where the autocratic method is used, (b), (c), and (d) might be advisable.

3. (c)—but your own character will suffer in the eyes of the group if you're not careful to do this honestly, without hypocrisy and without ramming people down each other's throats.

4. (b) 5. (b)

6. (c) Choice between the democratic or autocratic method would depend on the degree to which he seems to need reassurance. If you're in doubt, use the democratic approach first. If that fails to provide sufficient help, follow up by the autocratic method.

7. (b) But do it on the basis of its being a poor joke—rather than simply putting yourself in the role of wet blanket.

SCORING

Score each third of the quiz separately. Give yourself ten points for each correct answer. Rate your score by the following chart:

60–70 Outstanding
40–50 Good
20–30 Poor

Then compare the scores in each section. If your scores are generally low, or if they're lower than you want them to be in any one area, check back on the questions. They can help you get a better "feel" of the method of dealing with the attitude problems you're likely to face.

13 : *How to Build Communications*

ONE CHUTIST DEAD, 221 HURT IN CALLED-OFF DROP

You may have seen that headline. Behind it lay a story of communications that failed to click.

Scheduled for the Army's mammoth atomic war games in Texas was a practice combat jump by the 508th Airborne Regimental Combat team. But newspaper correspondents arriving at the jump area were told that the jump had been called off because of high winds.

Shortly thereafter, a headquarters teletype clattered out the news that the operation was under way. Officers not informed of the decision to cancel the maneuver had stuck to the original arrangements.

IT'S WAR!

Wartime or war games, failure of information channels can mean serious trouble.

In nonmilitary affairs, the complications may not be quite so grave. But haven't we all seen the crises or fiascos that result from communications breakdowns: the picnic that flops because half the group hasn't been told of a last-minute change in the location? The salesman out on the road, selling like crazy an item on which, for one reason or another, production has been suspended? The company which sets policy on a safety matter, then has to reverse itself when major accidents confirm the dissenting opinion of a foreman whose memo lies forgotten in the files?

In addition, much of the irritations and annoyance that people experience in their work can be traced to communications failures. And in many organizations, an over-all efficiency loss has the same origin, unrecognized though the fact may be.

DIAGNOSIS TROUBLE

"Nobody ever tells me anything!"

The person making that complaint might be—

subordinates down the line
your assistant
you yourself

It's fortunate if the thought *is* actually put into words. In that case, there's at least recognition that a communications sore spot exists. But, unfortunately, complaints about communications are rare. The reason is that symptoms of poor communications are slow to appear—and difficult to spot even when they do.

SHUT THAT DOOR

Behind most blocks to communication lies a basic error. It's the mistaken idea that communication in a group is like communication between two people, *except that there's more of it.*

That's the kind of thinking which explains the executive who assures you that he has no communications problems. "My door is always open," he says. *But all that comes in is a draft.* The fact that his subordinates don't cross the threshold fails to dent his self-satisfaction.

In the same way, you're likely to hear the "We're-one-big-happy-family" story. That's the line that many an executive takes when asked about his organization (including the exchange of ideas and information). Unfortunately, he forgets that many a so-called "happy family" has been thrown into a turmoil because teen-age Mary eloped with an unknown man—and "nobody had the faintest idea. . . ."

WHAT IS IT?

Before discussing communications further, let's get solid ground underfoot. What is—or are—communications anyway?

To begin with, it can be said that it's an area where more intelligent people flounder more sincerely than on almost any other subject you can name.

I recently attended a meeting of an advisory group which had as its purpose forming a human-relations program for a New York City educational institution. For one-half hour this group of experts discussed whether the word "communication" or "communications" should be used for one of the courses to be given.

Yes, that's right. The substance of this half-hour discussion was whether to use the word with or without an "s." And please remember, these people were extremely well versed in the subject at hand.

OUR AREAS OF IGNORANCE

Why was this group of highly qualified people, after half an hour's discussion, unable to get anywhere with what seems a minor point?

The fact is, *no one* can say whether the word should be spelled with or without an "s." The discussion at that meeting centered on the label for a bottle the contents of which are to some extent a mystery. It wasn't a question of whether the label was right or wrong. The question was—and is—could *any* label fit this bottle containing a largely unknown substance?

THE SIMPLEST COMMUNICATIONS SYSTEM

There are many areas in the field of communications we know nothing about. Fortunately, some things *are* known. It's possible, for example, to illustrate the difference between *communications* and *lack of communications.*

WATCH FOR THE BOWWOW

I have a little girl at home whose name is Vicki. When she was two, we tried to establish telephonic communications. She was very interested. She got up to the telephone, and her mother encouraged her to say something. At the other end of the phone, I'd say, "Hi, Vicki." But she didn't answer.

I exhausted the usual approaches, "Hi!" and "Do you hear me?' and "What did you have for breakfast?" Then I suddenly remembered a little trick that she had learned. I said, "Vicki, what kind of a noise does a doggy make?" Very faintly from the other end of the wire came "Bowwow."

There you have the difference between *communications* and *non-communications.* Until that little faint "bowwow" came from the other end of the wire, there was no communication. But the very instant I heard that little voice imitating a dog, communications had been established.

Note the importance of the response. A man shouting down a well is *not* communicating. Without something happening or changing, *without a result at the receiving end,* you can't realistically speak of communications at all.

Discount, therefore, the claims of the executive who proves he has excellent communications by showing you his slick-paper house organ, his periodic reports to employees, and so on. Ask him, rather, what indication he has that the material is being read, that it's *creating an effect* at the receiving end.

Now, what are the elements of the simple circuit established in the telephone talk with Vicki? It can be represented very easily:

This is the very simplest type of communications circuit involving two people. But don't be misled by the implied efficiency of that neat symbol. Just think of the obstacles which can arise in person-to-person contacts.

► *The personality problem.* A can't talk to B because "he's so shy, he won't open up"; or because "he talks so much, I couldn't get a word in edgewise."

► *Status problem.* There's the typist who's a conversational whirlwind among her sisters of the keys. When dealing with her boss, she turns tongue-tied.

► *Language problem.* "Marginal activity! Break-even point! Halo effect! I didn't understand a word of what he was saying."

Your leadership communications are subject to the entire list of face-to-face difficulties, plus the additional problems arising out of the complexities of the apparatus itself.

"ONE-TWO-THREE, TESTING"

It's simple enough to check a communications system—regardless of size. The answers to these questions will tell you how effective it is.

1. Does your communications setup permit *your people* to tell *you* all *you* need to know?

2. Does it permit *you* to tell *your people* all *they* need to know?

3. Does it permit *your people* to pass along necessary ideas, information, etc., to *each other*?

On the surface you have three simple questions to which the answers would seem easily available. But the fly in the ointment lies in the word *need*. What information and ideas, for example, do you *need* to get from your people? What ideas, information, etc., do your people *need* from you?

YOUR PERSONAL COMMUNICATIONS SYSTEM

The kind of communications system you select and develop should reflect the answers to the questions above.

It's possible to represent three systems available to you. The one you choose as a basic model—of course, you'd have to tailor the details to your specific needs—depends on the general nature of your leadership activity.

Autocratic communications. The basic path is from the leader directly to each individual.

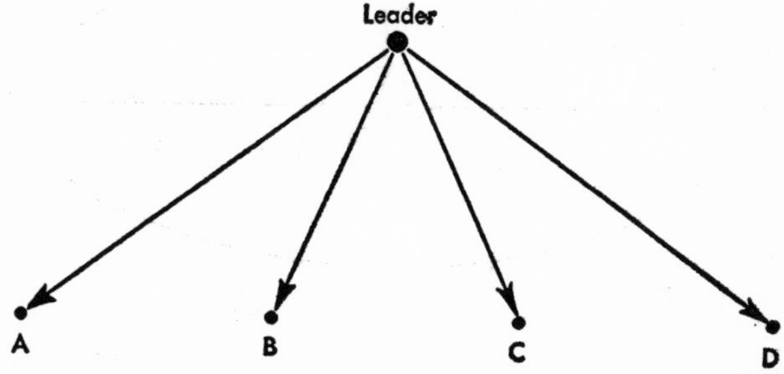

Although not indicated in the diagram, this point is also worthy of note: where side communications are necessary, they usually take place with the leader as middleman. In other words, to pass from group member A to group member B, a communication would proceed from A to the leader and then be passed along to B.

Advantages and disadvantages. Note that this system is relatively simple and streamlined. Its main advantage is speed. It's a fast system, to be used when you're under pressure or in a crisis situation.

Balanced against that main advantage is the handicap in the form of the tremendous burden on the shoulders of the man at the top. As the diagram shows, he is more or less isolated. Since his orders and directives are not necessarily discussed and explained by his subordinates, the effectiveness of his directives can only be learned on the basis of results. Sometimes those results can call for a change of method or plan. But with minimal "feedback," with generally poor return information—("Why should I tell that so-and-so anything?")—readjustments may be belated.

Democratic communications. The lines of communication between leader and group members are two-way. In actual

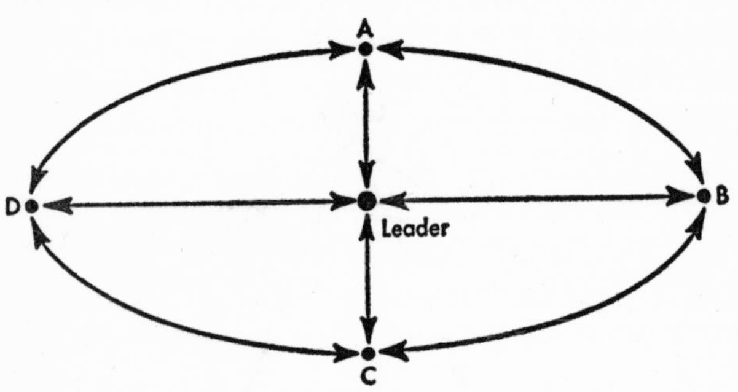

practice, this means that the democratic leader not only contacts group members for purposes of asking questions, making suggestions, passing along information, and so on, he also makes it possible—by personal contacts, prearranged conferences, other routine procedures—for group members to keep in touch with him.

Notice also that in this setup, side communications are

arranged for. Not only can group members contact you, it is possible for them to communicate with one another.

Advantages and disadvantages. The democratic method makes it possible to develop ideas. It's a unique feature of this communications system. It isn't necessary, for example, for the executive to think out a complete plan and then start the plan working by giving the necessary orders. The top man can begin with just a glimmer of an idea, or he may not even have the idea. He may just know that there is a problem. The democratic system makes it possible for him to bring the problem before the group. With the problem presented, there is not one brain but many working on the solution.

The second advantage is the greater emphasis placed on keeping the man at the top informed. The double heads on the arrows in the diagram indicate that a two-way flow takes place. The ideas go not only from executive to subordinates, but also from subordinates to the man at the top.

A disadvantage of this system is that when mishandled it becomes a time-waster and a depleter of energy. Just keep in mind the last conference you saw which got out of hand. The side talk, argument, and discussion beside the point demonstates what can happen to so-called "democratic" communications improperly controlled.

Free-rein communications. As the dotted lines indicate, the communications under free-rein leadership are at a minimum.

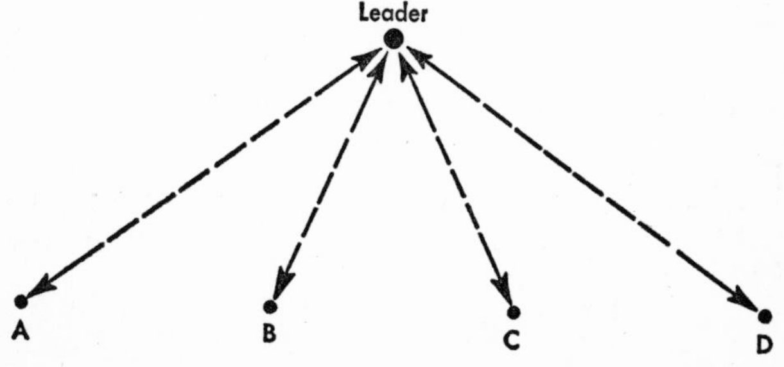

Under the free-rein method your subordinates are almost entirely on their own. The back-and-forth flow of ideas, suggestions, and consultations typical of the democratic system are almost entirely lacking.

Advantages and disadvantages. Advantages and disadvantages of the free-rein system are one and the same. It is a minimum communications hook-up. Where you want your people to operate undisturbed, this system has value. But substitute the word "undisturbed" for "in isolation" and the implications of the second phrase also point up the handicaps.

The system you use, the variations you adopt, will be determined by your specific needs. There are three additional aspects of communications to keep in mind in analyzing your requirements.

CHANNELS

Once you have decided in your own mind what system of communications is desirable or necessary, you must provide the *mechanical means* to implement the flow. Whether it's a matter of conferences or written reports, a matter of formal program review or informal face-to-face contacts, specific communications implements must become a standard part of the system.

Remember that merely having the desire to communicate is not enough. Consider the step taken by a company president interested in building democratic communications. He sent out the following interoffice memo to his supervisors on a matter of current company importance:

> Dear ——:
>
> Problem hours—slow starting, end-of-the-day lag, and so on—tend to increase during summer months. There is one point I would like to underline: problem hours tend to be contagious. They may start in one spot and spread

to another. For that reason, *interdepartmental teamwork* is often the best way to solve many of them.

Look into your own problem-hour situations. Figure out which of them could more readily be eased by co-operation with "the supervisor next door."

The answer may be a better tie-in of schedules, of exchanging work information in advance, or more efficient sharing of facilities. Whatever the specific problem-hour difficulty, discussions with your fellow supervisors can provide a solid basis for mutually satisfactory action.

Work out between yourselves the time and place of your meeting. If any personal scheduling problems remain unsolved, contact me.

Cordially,

J. B.

With this kind of encouragement, and *specific implementation,* the executive is likely to get the kind of side communications he's after.

QUANTITY OF COMMUNICATIONS

The amount of communications that exists is important. It can also be misleading. In the autocratic leadership method, for example, you will sometimes find a marked abundance of communications. Subordinates continually check back with their leader. They want more information, further instructions, and so on.

This situation may be explained, however, by the fact that there is more communications because there is more *dependence.* There is no rule that says an autocratic leader should not supply his subordinates with as much background information as they can intelligently absorb.

QUALITY

This is the third but probably most important question. In communications as well as in most other things, quantity, however vast, cannot make up for quality.

It's a fact underlined by the fate of many management suggestion systems. Where the system is poorly sponsored, where people get the idea that it's merely a stunt, and not actually a tool for getting ideas and participation, interest withers.

Unless your channels convey information that is informative (tell the kind of news they should know) and tell it clearly and interestingly, the communications job is not being done.

YOUR COMMUNICATIONS LEADERSHIP

You are responsible for the communications system in your group. Where the leader is communications-minded, grapevine, rumor factory, and so on, operate weakly. But the grapevine and other organization-harming systems flourish where the leader's communications effort lags.

The three basic approaches to leadership tend to develop different and specific communications systems. To see how well you function as a leader in the area of communications, answer the questions that follow. By comparing the scores of each part, you will see in which type of leadership role you are most successfully carrying out your communications responsibility. Implicit in your score is an evaluation of your present practices.

I. AUTOCRATIC COMMUNICATIONS

1. You feel that a situation has arisen which calls for a full-dress meeting of your group, with you slated to make

the main address. Trouble is, you're a poor speaker. Would your move be to—
(a) try to make the speech, regardless?
(b) have a capable subordinate make it?
(c) page Dale Carnegie?

2. The false rumor is spreading: "Mr. So-and-so is going to be canned because . . ." and the reason given may range from secretary-kissing to failing to marry the boss's daughter. You're Mr. So-and-so. Would you—
(a) do nothing?
(b) deny all the charges suggested as the reason for your removal?
(c) issue a written statement that you expect to be around for a long time to come?
(d) suggest to your superior that he issue such a statement in your behalf?

3. You succeed in tracing the rumor above, and find the originator to be a subordinate who has always cast a yearning eye at your job. Would you—
(a) fire him?
(b) warn him that any further out-of-line activity will mean his dismissal?
(c) discuss the circumstance with him, and try to make him see the error of his ways?

4. Someone in your group tells you that one of your subordinates is "bottlenecking communications around here. I've been giving him information which he should have—but hasn't—passed along to you." Assuming the charge is true, would you handle the situation by—
(a) defending your assistant?
(b) asking your assistant for his version of the affair?
(c) telling your informant to take up the problem with the assistant in question?

5. "I didn't understand your instructions," says one of your people. "Since I couldn't find you, I proceeded according to my own lights, and everything turned out fine." In such a case, would you—

(a) praise him for his ingenuity?
(b) give him hell for not going ahead with your orders, regardless?
(c) neither praise nor blame, but make the point that he should question orders he's uncertain about?

6. You're in a spot where you need ideas. You know the group can supply them, but you've never asked for their ideas before. Would you—
   (a) let the group know, by indirect means, that you'll be more receptive to their suggestions?
   (b) hire an "idea" man rather than ask the group for suggestions?
   (c) tell the group about the situation you're facing and ask for their help?
7. There's a change due which will hurt a few of your people. Doubts are troubling the entire group. Would you—
   (a) keep it under wraps until the last minute?
   (b) make a general announcement at once?
   (c) break it to the victims first, then to everybody else?
   (d) deny any change is contemplated in order to reassure the group?

ANSWERS

1. (b) is probably your best immediate move. (c) is probably a wise follow-up.

2. (a) This is one of the occasions when just sitting tight is extremely difficult, but advisable.

3. (c) Of course. (b) is tempting; but even though your chances of success aren't very high, you ought to take a crack at trying to weaken his hostility.

4. (b)

5. (c) The man in this situation is occasionally the fellow

who, consciously or otherwise, likes to "do things his own way." If you suspect you're dealing with a person of this type, and feel he's capable of making a contribution, it's probably wise to switch to the democratic method of dealing with him.

6. (c) The situation seems to call for a switch to the democratic approach in your handling of the group as a whole. But keep in mind that for consistency's sake, you'd probably have to make other adjustments in your leadership—in the area of implementation of their ideas, for example.

Number 7 is a tough communications problem for which no one approach has been found generally applicable. You'd have to weigh a number of intangibles—the manner in which the group as a whole would respond to an announcement of the facts, the relative number of individuals who will suffer, the actual extent of same, and so on. If you've chosen any solution but (d), give yourself full credit.

II. DEMOCRATIC COMMUNICATIONS

1. You get a request from your people: "There's been a lot of talk about mounting costs in running our division. Could we see the figures in black and white?" You're pretty sure your boss would veto any such proposal. Would you proceed to—
   (a) tell your boss of the request and try to overcome his objections to satisfying it?
   (b) tell your people, "Those figures can't be made available," and try to explain why on the basis of good business practice?
   (c) try to show the group it isn't necessary for them to have the figures in order to cut costs?
2. To see whether a routine informational report is really necessary, you stop sending it around. None of the people who customarily get it mention the omission. Would you—

(a) assume therefore that it is of no interest and discontinue it?
(b) examine the report to see whether it fulfills the purpose for which it was originally designed?
(c) dig back to the original purpose of the report and see whether that purpose is still valid?

3. You have been staging weekly meetings with your group. They were meant originally to be problem-solving conferences. Lately they have degenerated into gripe sessions. Would your way out be—
   (a) to discontinue them when a natural break comes up—a general summer vacation, for example?
   (b) call the shift to the attention of the group, and get them back on the track?
   (c) encourage the griping—if you feel you can tackle the causes thereafter?

4. Would you ever fire a person for spreading rumors?
   (a) Yes.
   (b) No.

5. Would you go out of your way—let's say a block out of your way—just to say hello to a subordinate you hadn't seen for a week or two?
   (a) Yes.
   (b) No.

6. At group meetings, X always hogs the floor whenever he can. Would you, accordingly,
   (a) to the best of your ability, keep him from getting the floor?
   (b) let him have his way?
   (c) try to develop other, more private, occasions for him to hold forth?

7. Do you always make it clear that the unpleasant information—layoffs, more restrictive regulations, for example—emanating from higher echelons have that source?
   (a) Yes.
   (b) No.

ANSWERS

1. (a) With all due deference to the sacred-cow treatment accorded cost matters in most management circles, it's probably true that in 50 per cent of the cases this information could be declassified without the slightest disadvantage. Just be realistic enough to expect a negative reaction from your superior, and be ready to adopt (b) as a second choice.

2. (c) 3. (c)

4. (a) Where there was malicious intent and harm done, it would probably be advisable. But note, backtracking a rumor to its source is difficult; and you should distinguish between the new rumor carrier, who passes it along, and the creator of the rumor.

5. (a) Usually, the further out of your way you go, the more appreciated is your effort.

6. (c)

7. (b) Frequently, your stature in the eyes of subordinates is measured by the extent to which you accept responsibility of this kind.

III. FREE-REIN COMMUNICATIONS

1. You have set up a routine of individual conferences by which you keep yourself informed of the progress your people are making. One man, however, is always postponing the meetings, otherwise putting you off. You decide his behavior amounts to bucking you. Would you—
   (a) have him submit written progress reports instead?
   (b) tell him you'll cancel all meetings, but he'll have to produce "results" at stated intervals?
   (c) recite the history of postponements, and ask him to explain them?
2. You've told one of your people something in confidence. Next day it's all over the place. Would you, as a *first* step—

(a) let him know that he's done himself irreparable damage in your eyes?
(b) let him know that you're pretty bitter about his indiscretion, but that it's water over the dam?
(c) ask him whether he is responsible for the news leak?

3. You learn that one of your group is taking his questions to one of his co-workers instead of to you. Would you—
   (a) ask him why?
   (b) let it pass, since he's getting correct information?
   (c) tell the man he's consulting to refuse to give him further information?
4. You learn that one of your group is taking questions to your superior that should be brought to you. Would you first—
   (a) ask him why?
   (b) try to figure out why?
   (c) give him to understand that you expect him to bring questions within your province to you—or else?
5. One of your people comes to you with the suggestion that periodic group conferences be held. You explain that the nature of the work makes them inadvisable, but he says, "I still think it would be nice if we could get together occasionally." Would you—
   (a) repeat your explanation that under the conditions of work, conferences would be ill-advised?
   (b) start thinking about arranging social get-togethers after hours?
   (c) have the meetings if you found others felt the same way?
6. You request each group member to submit written progress reports. But the reports come in late, garbled, and are worth very little. Would you—
   (a) shift to oral reports instead?
   (b) insist on more cooperation in the matter?
   (c) simplify the report form?

7. Can communications be *too* good? A member of the group bombards you with an endless succession of notes, reports, and inter-office memos. The output is distinguished *only* by its quantity. Would you—
   (a) discourage them?
   (b) let 'em come, without doing too much about them?
   (c) answer them as well as you could?
   (d) look for some basic situation that was troubling the man?

ANSWERS

1. (b) 2. (c)

3. (b) Your role of free-rein leader requires a minimum of interference. If your subordinate finds it advisable to consult a colleague, you shouldn't interfere. But some study of the situation to learn why he sidesteps you is in order.

4. (b) The reasoning is similar to that of question 3.

5. (b) If your subordinates feel the need for group contact, it's a good idea to provide it under circumstances which best assist—or least interfere with—the work.

6. (c) 7. (d)

SCORING

Score each section of the quiz separately. Give yourself ten points for each correct answer. Rate yourself according to the following chart:

60 – 70	Outstanding
40 – 50	Good
20 – 30	Poor

Your score in each of the three sections provides a rule-of-thumb approximation of weak and strong points in the communications-building area of your leadership.

14 : *How to Increase Group Effectiveness*

What per cent of your subordinates' capacities are actually reflected in their work?

10 per cent?

50 per cent?

90 per cent?

One foreign industrial expert has stated, "In Europe we use 5 per cent of our employees' ability. In the United States, the average is about 20 per cent."

Let's assume the 20 per cent figure is low. Let's say that for your subordinates, efficiency is *twice* as high. That still leaves plenty of room for improvement.

But—can the improvement be made?

The ordinary incandescent light bulb, for example, is only about 2.5 per cent efficient. Room for improvement? Plenty. But practical considerations stand in the way. A more efficient bulb *could* be constructed by using finer-gauge filaments—but there'd also be a shortening of bulb life and a lessening of general durability.

Practical difficulties likewise hamstring some of the methods that seem to hold out promise of increasing the effectiveness of people. Consider these two situations:

► By working closely with one of your subordinates, you feel you might raise his effectiveness 10 per cent. You'd *still* be faced by the question as to whether that return would be worth while in terms of your *own* time and effort.

► You find you can arrange the work so that Jim Jones, who's at his best in the morning, does the more demanding parts of his job then, the routine later. His general level of improvement would jump. But that particular schedule might not tie in well with the activities of Jim Jones's associates, possibly bring down *their* level of accomplishment.

OVERLOAD?

There's another point that needs to be made. During World War II, I was a supervisor in the Celanese Plastics Division, Newark, New Jersey. One of the pieces of equipment placed in my charge was a spiral wrapper, a machine with a personality all its own. At times it would perform beautifully. At others, the girls operating the machine were reduced to tears at its nip-ups.

One day, egged on by a tight production schedule, I suggested to Agnes, my star operator, that we increase the motor speed by about 20 per cent. Agnes didn't like the idea and said so. She wouldn't have time to feed the machine, count the tubes, clean up, and so on. Over her protests, I persuaded her to make the trial.

The first attempt was fine. The spiral tubing came sliding off the wrapping mandrel at a definitely accelerated rate.

Then the fun began. The automatic saw that cut the tubing into lengths began to miss. The tube, unhindered, snaked swiftly across the floor. The stand holding the pan of adhesive started to shake, then crashed, splashing its contents far and wide. The roll of plastic material flew off the loading spindle and bounded away.

Agnes shut off the machine and looked at me accusingly. Words, needless to say, were unnecessary.

Her viewpoint was reinforced by our maintenance engineer with whom I discussed the incident that afternoon. "Every machine has a best speed," he told me. "It's just as true of that spiral wrapper as it is of an automobile. You drive your car at sixty, and she's headed for the junk heap a lot sooner. And you'll have plenty of maintenance headaches in the meantime."

That spiral wrapper going haywire is probably as close as you can get to a mechanical version of a nervous breakdown. The parallel between the machine and people is clear.

Don't confuse *output* with *effectiveness*. We must rule out increased output gained at the expense of fatigue, poorer quality of performance, or other complications.

What we're talking about in this chapter is not how to get more work out of subordinates by putting them under greater pressure. Our aim is to explore the possibilities of improving individual efficiency without forcing their pace, or creating undue strains or tensions.

REMOVING THE ROADBLOCKS

You get a pretty good idea of the depth of the problem from the comment made by an industrial executive I interviewed. He had made a name for himself in his organization through his success with this precise problem—the fuller utilization of human resources.

"I can't formularize my method," he said. "If I could, I'd become the most outstanding industrialist in the country overnight."

You can safely go along with that statement. There is certainly no sure-fire formula.

Paradoxically, the problem is tough *not* because there is *little* possibility for remedial action, but because so *many* possibilities exist. Whether you're planning their work or building their morale, *most* of the things you do in relation to your people affect their efficiency.

In addition to your general leadership methods, certain steps tend to have a direct influence on the efficiency problem. The extent to which these steps pay off depends on your skill in adapting them to your special needs.

The most fruitful approach is likely to be one based on this fact: *the potential for greater effectiveness for the most part already exists.* In other words, you're not trying to *build* effectiveness. You *are* trying to make better use of something that's already there. The logical answer, then, seems to be to *find the obstacles to effectiveness,* and to *take action that will remove or minimize them.*

Here are three fertile areas for your consideration.

1. **Internal Obstacles.** Your subordinates tend to lose effectiveness because of resentments, or other feelings of dissatisfaction with their treatment. These are the words you sometimes hear which express these underlying feelings:

► *Favoritism.* "The harder you work the less brains they think you have. It's the guy who plays up to the boss that gets booted up the ladder."

► *Inadequate reward.* "Why should I kill myself on this job? I'm not getting enough for it."

► *Lack of recognition.* "My boss doesn't even know I'm alive."

► *Meaningless job.* "As far as I can tell, my job is just a high-grade kind of boondoggle."

In each of the above cases, analyzing the symptom of itself suggests a cure. The leader, for example, who knows a subordinate is holding back because he feels his efforts are not receiving sufficient recognition can take the steps in his dealings with that individual which will overcome that attitude.

2. **Procedural Obstacles.** Your people can be hampered by their failure to go along with regular procedures. They may stretch out rest periods, dawdle at starting time.

In an ordinary business or factory situation this element

generally is the signal for closer supervision. And there's little doubt that the supervisory aspect of leadership can have a large effect in this area. Consider, for instance, the following points which represent more or less your "supervisory" function. They come into play in the actual day-to-day activity of your people.

Take the single problem of the subordinate who "can't get started" in his job. Half an hour after he should have begun, he's still "preparing"—straightening out unnecessarily, or engaged in other activities that substitute for effective action.

Here's where your own personal influence can come in. You might arrange your own starting activities along these lines:

► Is the assignment "scaring him off"? You can help him get organized by showing him how to lay out each step systematically and control the physical setup.

► Is the assignment unattractive? That may be unavoidable, but you can make it more pleasant by pointing out possible short cuts, openings for improvement.

SELF-STARTERS

Your close attention at the start is not the only answer. It *can't* be, since you can't always be there. And it *shouldn't* be, since as far as is practicable, getting started should be the responsibility of the man himself.

Handled with care, these tools help build that responsibility:

Deadlines. By fixing the end of the job, you set up a certain amount of pressure at the beginning. But note that where a deadline is unreasonable, it can turn out to be a headache instead of a help.

Leeway on how to do the job. Clearly, this is risky with the beginner; he may need help at any point along the line. But with the more experienced person, the opportunity to use his own judgment can serve as a spur—while too much direction can act as a drag.

Responsibility for reporting difficulties. In some cases, there's no way out of it; you'll have to check up. But again with your more qualified people, it's often better to hand them the ball. Otherwise the group as a whole may develop the habit of waiting for you to make the rounds.

The extent to which you desire this backtracking will depend in part on whether you use the autocratic, democratic, or free-rein approach as your *general* leadership method.

LAST-LAP LAG

Your people may be losing effectiveness because of tapering or easing off toward the end of an assignment. Here are some of the problems you face:

► *The man who "can't finish up."*

His assignment can't be completed by quitting time. Therefore, why start?

If you hear this thought expressed—or suspect it underlies a drop in effort—consider:

The tailored assignment. Can you break down or divide the individual's task so that it has a natural cutoff point that hits close to the end of the day?

The helping hand. Can you provide him with assistance that will ensure completion of the task? That sometimes suggests "doubling up." Occasionally, it could mean your own participation.

This step, incidentally, will tend to put group pressure on individuals who are not carrying their full share of the load. No one likes to be Bill in this complaint: "Just because Bill was stalling, we've got to step in and do his job for him."

► *The individual who's "saving it for tomorrow."*

The assignment *could* be finished. But why do it? Might as well save it and have something to start on in the morning.

Against this attitude, you can use these alternatives: Keep posted on actual finishing time. You know the capacity of your people; you know the approximate completion time of their assignments. If it's necessary, check up around deadline time. See for yourself how the job's going. If the size of your group makes this difficult, have *them* contact *you* as they finish up.

3. **The "social" obstacle.** There have been many studies of the relationship between an individual's performance and his group adjustment. One of the more interesting investigations was made in England, and involved a group of 350 West Indians who had migrated into the country in 1941–1943.

Most of them adjusted well to their job life in the English war factories. Some didn't. Anthony H. Richmond, of the Department of Social Science in the University of Liverpool, set out to discover whether there was any relationship between (a) the *performance* of these workers, and (b) their *adjustment* to their job surroundings—the way they got along with each other and with the company.

The conclusions were revealing: the workers who were *most* at home in their jobs were also those who *did best*. And those who were least at home in their jobs were those who did worst.

CREATING A SOCIAL ATMOSPHERE

Here again, your choice of general leadership method—autocratic, democratic, or free rein—is one of the major factors. The better suited your method is to the kind of people you have in your group, the better adjustment they will make. There are a number of other factors which tend to bear on individual cases:

► *Feuds.* Frictions of long standing between individuals obviously prevent a satisfactory adjustment. And what starts as an individual loss in effectiveness can encompass the entire group, if the situation is permitted to fester.

► *Cliques.* The social bars a group sometimes builds for itself can short-circuit communications, hamper cooperation.

► *The goat.* Occasionally, a single person can become the target for the hostility or aggressive feelings of the group. Interestingly enough, individuals under this kind of attack sometimes try to fight back to compensate for the undesirable social role in which they've been put, by turning in an outstanding performance. But even here, the end results are likely to be undesirable, because the group, in turn, intensifies its aggressions.

The difficulty in this situation is to protect the scapegoat effectively without deepening the rift in group unity. In many cases, the manifest unfairness of the situation can be used to ease the aggressions. Another method that has some merit is to crack down hard on the rule violations that usually go hand in hand with the undesirable conduct—horseplay, for example.

Keep in mind, then, that the sum of the things you do to help your subordinates adjust to their colleagues—introductions for new people, creating the opportunities for socializing, and so on—from the long view, can improve their effectiveness.

TESTING YOUR SKILL

The following self-test gives you some idea of how well you handle the human resources at your disposal. The pin-pointed situations can help you assess your judgments in this important leadership function. Make your answers in terms of what you *have* done, or feel you actually do in the situations given.

I. AUTOCRATIC LEADERSHIP

1. A member of your group, with a strong sense of rivalry toward you, forms a clique which tries to block achievement of the goals you set. If you have no doubt of his intentions, would you—
   (a) fire him?
   (b) make him your assistant?
   (c) break up the clique by shifting the individuals around?
   (d) tell him, in effect, that you know what he's up to, but as long as he does his work satisfactorily, it's O.K. with you?
2. You get this story from a group member: "I've worked in a lot of places before, but I've never been expected to work as hard." Would you—
   (a) tell him he can leave if he's dissatisfied?
   (b) ask him to back up his statement with facts?
   (c) find out whether what he really meant was that he was working harder than he was able?
3. You hear from somebody: "Joe Jones is a slick operator. He's doing such an outstanding job just to get in good with you." Would you—
   (a) fire Joe?
   (b) reprimand your informant?
   (c) tell your informant, "Let everybody know that Joe is achieving his purpose. And anybody else can do likewise by adopting Joe's method"?
4. Is your highest award (advancement or other sign of approval) generally given to the man who—
   (a) does the best job?
   (b) tries the hardest?
   (c) has shown the greatest personal loyalty to you?
5. You find there's a difference in group effort when you're present and when you're not. Would you—

(a) try to discover who the principal slackers are?
(b) make it your business to stick around when the group's at work?
(c) put more emphasis on accomplishment, work goals, meeting deadlines, and so on?

6. Whom would you commend most highly: the man who—
   (a) succeeds, despite handicaps, in doing a job?
   (b) is always helping the other fellow?
   (c) sacrifices self-interest for the sake of group achievement?
7. Two of your group are caught smoking—a serious infraction of rules. One is a female; the other a male. Would you—
   (a) punish both equally?
   (b) punish neither, in order to be fair?
   (c) punish the man more severely?

ANSWERS

1. (d) You strengthen your leadership position and weaken his standing by calling the turn.

2. (c)

3. (c) That's the old Lincoln approach and it worked with Grant.

4. (a)

5. (c) In a situation of this kind, long-range measures are indicated.

6. (a) 7. (a)

II. DEMOCRATIC LEADERSHIP

1. You call a meeting of your subordinates to discuss a storage problem. It degenerates into a round of bickering, charges and countercharges of space hogging, and so on. Would you—

(a) give each man a chance to justify his own position?
(b) eject the noisiest?
(c) elect a committee to find out what the storage situation is at present?

2. One of your group tells you, "I like Pete X personally. But he's so slow he hampers me in my work." Would you—
(a) ask Pete what's slowing him up?
(b) discuss the problem with your superior?
(c) dig into the matter to learn the background?

3. You get the complaint: "Joe Y isn't doing his job and is pulling down our group performance as a result." If this confirms your own observations, would you—
(a) try to get rid of Joe Y, by transfer or dismissal?
(b) discuss the matter with Joe?
(c) discuss the matter with your superior?

4. You find your group dividing into two camps. Embarrassingly enough, you yourself are at the core of the controversy. The faction favoring you numbers about the same as those opposed. Would you—
(a) try to win over the *con's* by favoring them over the *pro's*?
(b) try to rectify in yourself the quality that's causing the split—whether you think it's being fair to yourself or not?
(c) take up the problem with your superior?
(d) take up the problem with the ringleader of the *con's*?

5. One of your employees convinces you that a company policy is "taking the heart out" of the group and thereby blocking its unstinted effort. Would you—
(a) wink at observance of the policy, since the result will be better group performance?
(b) try to sell the group on the policy, regardless of your personal feelings, because that's the course loyalty to the company dictates?
(c) consult your superior?

6. One of your people is shy, lacks self-confidence, and doesn't join in group discussions. Would you—
   (a) try to build his self-confidence by assuring him, in private conversation, that he's as capable a speaker as anyone in the group?
   (b) try to steer a discussion around a subject you know he has well in hand, and then toss the ball his way?
7. A new employee comes to you and says: "I'm trying to do a job here, but several of the fellows have been telling me to ease off or else. What shall I do?" Would you—
   (a) fire him for the sake of restoring harmony to the group?
   (b) let the group know they either match the newcomer's performance or they're through?
   (c) try to analyze the factors that account for this superior performance?
   (d) try to stimulate the group to match his performance?

ANSWERS

1. (c)
2. (c) It's wise to check any such statement before taking action.
3. (b) It's always a good idea to learn what's behind a so-called "fact" on which may hinge a decision with a built-in kickback.
4. (d) The (b) choice is a tempting solution because it seems to be an easy out. Trouble is, a situation of this kind is usually deep-seated. As soon as one course of friction is removed, two spring up in its place. For that reason, it's generally your strongest move to put your cards on the table with the opposition.
5. (c) 6. (b)
7. Either (c) or (d), depending on specific circumstances.

III. FREE-REIN LEADERSHIP

1. You disagree completely with the line of activity one of your people is following toward an assigned objective. You grant that the disagreement is basically a matter of opinion. Would you—
   (a) let him follow his own inclinations?
   (b) pressure him into adopting the direction you prefer?
   (c) compromise on a course between the two opposed ideas?
2. One of your people refuses to come to you with his problems, even though he's pretty well stymied. He says he'd rather "muddle through it in my own fashion." Would you—
   (a) permit him to follow this course?
   (b) try to help him resolve the difficulties?
   (c) let him know that either he comes to you with his problems or he's in for trouble?
3. One of your people is clearly trying to take on the role of informal leader. His actions are limited to such steps as speaking up for the group, trying to organize their activities outside the limits of the work, and so on. Would you—
   (a) do what you can to remove him, if it can be accomplished gracefully?
   (b) step out, and let him run things?
   (c) accept him as informal leader to the extent of recognizing, for example, that he does speak for the group in some matters?
4. One of your group tells you: "You've assigned me to a job I don't like. Why don't you have the new man do it?" Would you—
   (a) adopt his suggestion?
   (b) fire him on the spot?
   (c) tell him why he was selected for the assignment and *insist* that he do it?

5. Your efforts to get employee X to cooperate with employee Y on a mutual problem are fruitless. They refuse for personal reasons. You realize you've made a mistake in trying to throw them together. Would you—
   (a) insist that they obey orders?
   (b) have a three-way talk to settle the feud?
   (c) take up the matter in separate talks with each?
   (d) let the matter drop, since you can hand the job to two other employees?
6. Would you give your most enthusiastic people the most trying jobs?
   (a) Yes.
   (b) No.
7. Would you give your least enthusiastic people the least demanding jobs?
   (a) Yes.
   (b) No.

ANSWERS

1. (a) It's typical of free-rein leadership that the leader largely follows a hands-off policy. If this policy is impractical, the leader should not be using the free-rein approach.

2. (b) 3. (c)

4. (c) Using the free-rein approach *does not* mean you fail to assert authority when necessary.

5. Either (b) or (c), depending on the degree to which the feud is explosive.

6. (a)

7. (b) The difference between questions 6 and 7 is this: implicit in the course suggested in 6. (a) is the reward of satisfaction in polishing off a tough job. But to give the easier jobs to the weaker group members as a matter of policy would be an unfair distribution of the work.

SCORING

Score each section of this quiz separately. Give yourself 10 points for each question you have answered correctly. Then rate yourself according to the following chart:

60 – 70	Outstanding
40 – 50	Good
20 – 30	Poor

Comparing the scores you have made in each section will show you where your strong and weak points lie.

MORE POWER TO YOU

15 : *Your Daily Work Schedule*

Minute by minute, hour by hour, what does a leader do, how does he go about his job of leading? When is he being effective, when is he falling flat on his face?

One man may be making his most effective efforts leaning back in his swivel chair, feet on the desk, thinking.

Another's greatest triumphs may be measured by the drops of perspiration coursing down his face, the sheer energy expended guiding his group through a crisis.

The content of your leadership job—what you actually do in the course of your work—can provide an excellent insight into your over-all effectiveness.

LEADER-FOLLOWER ACTIVITY

The manager of a New York department store stopped to chat with an old-time employee.

"How are things, John?"

"Not too good. . . ." And the old-timer went into detail: he'd lost a sales slip, been forced to put up with the didoes of an unreasonable customer, wasn't getting items he needed from the stock department.

"Funny thing," commented the executive to a friend later on, "old John was as fussed up as *I'd* have been if I'd mislaid our weekly sales report, had an argument with the chairman of the board, and failed to get delivery from our suppliers."

IS IT DIFFERENT?

Is there anything special about a leader's job? Are his headaches different from those of anyone with any other kind of job to do? It's a good question, because it can start a revealing and helpful analysis of your leadership activity.

To begin with, compare the job objectives in these three related cases:

► A roll operator has the task of turning out 900 pounds of molding powder from his mixing rolls during one shift.

► The shift foreman is after 20,000 pounds of powder from his crew in the course of the shift.

► The divisional superintendent is seeking a yield of 60,000 pounds daily from the roll room.

It's clear that the problem of goal achievement for the superintendent in this case is similar to that of his subordinates. *But note the difference in degree.* The rank-and-file individual goal can be stated in terms of hundreds. For the man running the works, the ante reaches tens of thousands.

The goal of the leader is usually a total or final goal. The objectives of his subordinates usually have the nature and magnitude of subgoals.

The above point does not lessen the importance of the subordinates' efforts. On the contrary, it demonstrates the *dependence* of the leader on his people. The leader's accomplishment is usually *the sum total of the achievements of his group.*

What you do on the job, then, should be aimed at helping along group achievement—removing the roadblocks, straightening out the tangles, smoothing the way.

YOUR DAILY DOZEN

According to one observer, the leader's contributions toward the achievements of his group are:

to plan the work that's to be done;

to decide in what order the work should be done;

to select people to do the work;

to tell them why it needs doing;

to tell them how to do it;

to tell them when to do it;

to listen to reasons why it can't be done, or should be done by somebody else, or done in a different way, or at another time;

etc., etc.

There's the rebuttal for the man who, trying for an easy out, proclaims, "The leader's job is to lead." But when you get right down to brass tacks, the "leading" turns out to be not a single thing, but a highly complex series of functions. While the list above indicates some of a leader's activities, it's far from being the whole story.

ARE YOU ON SCHEDULE?

What you do on the job in terms of your own personal activity is important for several reasons:

(a) It sets a tone, a tempo of activity for the group as a whole.

(b) It is often used by subordinates as a model for their own activity.

But even more important:

(c) The nature of your activity can reveal *to what extent you're actually applying the leadership approach you have selected.*

For example: the editor-in-chief of a nationally distributed publication had chosen the free-rein approach as best for handling his staff. He actually *thought* he was leading his group by the free-rein method.

But the fact was, *fully half his time was devoted to conferences and discussions with his subordinates*. The point is, *not* that he was wrong to do so, but that if his people required that much help and guidance, then the free-rein method was *not* well suited to his needs.

With considerations of this kind in mind, a brief study of your daily work schedule can show you whether—

► you're carrying out in practice the general leadership method you've decided to use;

► you're adequately satisfying the leadership needs of your group;

► your daily moves show a weakness in your self-scheduling.

And lastly, if you feel it's desirable, one additional step can—

► show you how to work out an efficient schedule for your daily routines.

SCHEDULING YOUR WORK?

There are plenty of good reasons that can be advanced *against* blueprinting leadership activity.

For one thing, the nature of your work is not likely to be cyclical or repetitive. Each week generally brings a series of new and unforeseen duties. And this element of unpredictability is certainly a good and major reason for avoiding a rigid schedule of your activities.

Yet the alternatives to planning your daily work may have undesirable consequences. Here, for example, are some of the stock answers a number of people in leadership positions gave to the question, "How do you decide what you do next on your job?"

"I do the thing *most recently* called to my attention."

"I tackle the job on which there is *most pressure* for completion."

"I find I do the thing that I *do best.*"

"I do the thing that I *do worst.*"

"I do the think I *like most.*"

It's pretty clear that the cumulative results of any of these approaches are likely to be far from satisfactory.

THE PSYCHOLOGICAL HURDLE

There's another obstacle. Even if logic eventually persuades you of the desirability of self-scheduling, you will probably still hesitate. Don't be surprised. Many people resist the kind of self-examination that may mean change of current behavior.

There may be an unwillingness to face the facts brought to light. For example, you may be spending too many hours doing things *you instinctively want to continue,* even though they don't represent the best use of your time.

There's some resistance to change in most of us. Yet, since improvement necessarily means change, consider seriously going through the steps that will give you the information you need to evaluate and reapportion your work time.

THE SELF TIME-STUDY SHEET

The first step requires that you make a record of your present time allocation, of the way you do your job right now.

Begin by making a simple chart consisting of one column for each day in the week that you work. If it's five days, you will have five columns, headed respectively, Monday, Tuesday, Wednesday, Thursday, Friday.

Now proceed as follows:

► Select a normal work week. If it isn't truly representative of your activity, the information will be misleading. In certain cases it may be advisable to keep a record for several weeks.

► Keep the chart on hand so that you can note down each time expenditure you make.

► Make your notations as soon as possible after a particular task is finished. If you find your time tends to be broken up into very short periods of activity, it may be advisable to make the entries once every hour.

► Don't overlook small items. A number of five-minute jobs can account for a big chunk of working time.

► Break down a complex task into its individual elements. One continuous activity may consist of several different kinds of work. For example, making out a report may require ordering forms, getting information from various group members, checking facts on your own.

► Note the starting and stopping time of each activity. For example:

"9:00 to 9:30—Reading incoming correspondence."

"9:30 to 9:45—Conferring with Mr. Smith about the equipment problem."

Keep your time-study chart as accurately as possible for an entire week. When you have done this, you're ready for the next step.

THE JOB-BREAKDOWN CHART

First of all, the data you have collected has to "add up" in the literal sense. Take your first day's record, for instance, and total the time of the individual items.

Does the sum clearly total hours of your work day? If not, your record is either inaccurate or incomplete. You may have left out something, or underestimated time spent on indi-

JOB BREAKDOWN CHART

Contacts With Subordinates					Procedural Matters				Line and Staff Contacts			
Training and Instruction	Work Assignment and Discussion	General Personnel Matters	"Social" Contacts	Other	Review-ing Work Done	Improving Methods	Planning Work	Other	Reports	Conferences and Interviews	Contacting Other Departments	Other

vidual jobs. In that case, you will have to correct your time-study data.

Check through each day in the same manner. Fill in, if you can, any omissions. If you can't do so accurately, it's better to check yourself on another day—preferably the same day of the week. Your next step is to redistribute the data from your personal time-study to a chart similar to the one above.

ANALYZING THE DATA

After you have totaled the time under each heading in the Job Breakdown Chart, examine your results with this question in mind: "Is the time desirably balanced?"

This is the question that can act as an objective measure of your leadership activity. If, for example, as with the editor mentioned earlier, you find considerable time devoted to conferences and discussions with subordinates, regardless of other indications, it is *not* likely that you're using the free-rein approach. Here are some additional tips:

Planning. If a large amount of your time is spent in laying out the work of subordinates in detail, it's likely that your general approach is an autocratic one. Is that what you want?

Conferences and interviews. If you spend a relatively small amount of time conferring with your people, it is not likely that you're using the democratic approach. Is that what you want?

Using this same questioning approach for the various items in the chart can help you decide whether you're actually practicing the leadership method you think you are.

REDISTRIBUTING YOUR TIME

If you like, you can use your time-study analysis to work out a new schedule for yourself. If you do, keep in mind this important point: your scheduling should not be on a theoretical basis. Your objective should be to have your schedule *reflect the functions which your leadership job makes advisable and necessary.*

Rescheduling has this advantage: it can help remove some standard obstacles to efficiency. Lost or wasted time may result from duplicating the work of a subordinate. In some cases, time waste may result from walking about from one part of your area to another.

Interruptions may largely be unnecessary or controllable. Phone answering, for example, may be turned over to a subordinate; reception of and conducted tours for visitors may also be a time waste which you can eliminate by delegation.

Your time-study data should reveal such weak spots. Frequently, just knowing what you're doing wrong suggests its own remedy.

16 : *Responsibility and Delegation*

According to Nietzsche, "Life always gets harder toward the summit—the cold increases, responsibility increases."

Most will agree that responsibility is one of the "hard" parts of life at the top of the ladder. Usually overlooked is the reason. Actually, there are two sources of trouble:

The semantic difficulty. Responsibility is too often thought of as a single thing. This is an oversimplified view that makes for confusion and bewilderment because it's *contrary to reality*.

The practical difficulty. Responsibility consists of a *play of forces* which beat upon the leader, *sometimes pushing him several ways at once.*

THE PATTERN OF RESPONSIBILITY

Leadership responsibility is complex because it encompasses four different, and sometimes conflicting, allegiances:

Your individual subordinates. To the extent that they are members of your group, you owe them protection, help, and guidance.

Your group. The progress and well-being of the group are your direct concern. In disciplining an individual who breaks rules, for example, your purpose is partly to defend the group. An executive who takes up with his superior a policy that he feels is bad for his people is acting to improve group well-being.

The organization. Your group may be part of a larger unit. Whether it's a company, a club, or any other kind of organization, frequently you act out of consideration for its welfare. That's why an executive may feel it necessary to take action against an individual for "the good of the company."

Yourself. It exists in fact, but seldom arises in the course of discussion: the leader has a responsibility toward himself, his own sense of status, principles, dignity, and integrity.

For example, a subordinate's breach of discipline may not be serious in itself. But you may have to use your authority to keep him in line, and thereby safeguard your prestige and future relations with the group.

WHEN THE PRESSURES DON'T BALANCE

From time to time, you find yourself in a situation where the confusion of allegiances isn't easily resolved. And then the going can get really rough.

Let's say Jane Jones, president of a parent-teacher group, has the responsibility of selecting a member of the group for a particularly desirable assignment.

Her friend Helen Doe very much wants the plum. An "enemy," Frances Roe, would probably do the job better.

How should Jane make the choice? Is her responsibility toward the group more important than her feelings for Helen Doe, and against Frances Roe?

Sure, you'll say. No question about it. But what if she knows that her failure to appoint Helen will gain her Helen's ill-will, and the possibility that Helen will leave the group? Helen's resignation, let's say further, would be a loss to the group, and would disturb morale.

There's no limit to the number of considerations you can

add to this kind of situation. Each factor will tend to throw the balance of responsibility first one way, then the other.

How can you evaluate situations of this kind? Of course, the standard guides apply here: fairness, consistency, a logical balancing of the pros and cons of the given case. And then, for the democratic leader, there is the device of getting the group, or even the individuals most concerned with the situation, to join in making the choice.

However, in many instances, the four aspects of your responsibility are so related as to dictate a relatively clear action. See how this fact holds for the following cases.

BALANCING YOUR RESPONSIBILITIES

Usually, all four obligations—to the individual, group, parent organization, and yourself—have a bearing in any given situation. By helping the individual, for example, you ultimately help the group, the company, and yourself.

But in most cases, *one* of the four purposes is primary. And it shapes both your decision and the way you implement it.

Suppose you're an employer. You find that one of your people can't do the job for which he was hired. You let him go—because your primary purpose is the welfare of the company.

In another case, a man is having difficulty performing certain parts of his job. He is imposing a heavier burden on your group as a whole—but you are confident that he will make good with more training. You push into the background the discomfort to the group, and focus on the other purpose—helping him. You may even use your authority to quiet any criticism of the man that comes from the group.

But don't overlook the fact that frequently conflicts among your four areas of responsibility are only *temporary*. Occasionally you may be called on to make a decision that *seems* to favor one purpose above another. But considered from the long view, *they tend to become identical.* What benefits one will, in most cases, benefit all.

You would be doing an employee an actual disservice, for example, by keeping him in a job for which he wasn't suited. He faces no rosy future, and certainly he isn't likely to find much satisfaction in his daily work.

ESCAPE?

It's only natural that leaders, consciously or unconsciously, often try to get out from under the responsibility burden. Unfortunately, there's no known way to do this. Two much-used methods invariably end up in disaster:

Buck-passing. The attempt to palm off one's responsibility on someone else—either superior or subordinate—invariably weakens a leader's position.

Delegation. The leader who uses the procedures of delegation as a means of *lightening responsibility* is bound to face eventual kickbacks, as the fact that he *cannot* shift his basic responsibility clashes with his hopes.

WHAT DELEGATION IS

Delegation is an extremely vital technique for the leader to cultivate. Misused, looked on as an escape hatch through which the leader can lessen responsibility, it's bound to kick back. But delegation used as a means of *better meeting your responsibilities* can mean your salvation.

There's a single basic fact that makes delegation a necessity. It is that *your responsibility in almost all cases is greater than your personal capacity to carry it out.*

No one expects a company president to personally produce, package, and sell his product. What he is expected to do—

and must do in his leadership capacity—is to concentrate on the essentials, turn over the handling of less important details to others.

WHEN TO DELEGATE

Your responsibilities tend to develop and change. New problems come up and make new demands on your time. You must be ready to make corresponding changes in the tasks you reserve for yourself and those you assign to others.

Situations like these can be eased through delegation:

1. **When you're overburdened.** You have twenty reports to go through and time only for ten. You either have to delegate the entire job of report screening to a subordinate, have him give you the gist of each one, or read the ones you can cover yourself, turn over the less important ones to him to be read, digested, and summarized for you.

2. **In emergencies.** Occasionally, you're faced by a series of problems which have to be tackled all at once. No matter how pressing each may be, regardless of the fact that ordinarily you have handled each one personally, you may still have to delegate some if the time element is important.

3. **In your absence.** Whether it's a vacation or out-of-town business, someone has to provide a minimum amount of control while you're gone.

DELEGATION "DON'TS"

Certain situations make it impossible for you to delegate, no matter how much you might like to do so:

1. **Lack of qualified subordinates.** If you have no one willing or capable of shouldering the secondary responsibilities of the delegated job, you're stuck. You may be able to get through by constant checking back of a person who's willing but not

quite capable. Even so, you're losing a good deal of the time-saving value of delegation.

2. **The hot potato.** Don't make the mistake of passing along a problem to a subordinate which you yourself feel unable to handle. Consult with others, yes; but don't expect a subordinate to make a decision for which you will then hold him responsible, when you yourself are incapable of making it. It's not merely a matter of decision-making. There are actions which take on full meaning and weight *only* when performed by the leader.

Gen. Matthew B. Ridgway, during his campaign in Korea, displayed a personal courage that many considered foolhardy. He placed himself at advanced outposts, exposed himself to the enemy's artillery and small-arms fire. His justification was simple: "There are times when a man leading other men has got to be at the danger spot. That's where he can make the difference between victory and defeat."

3. **The power to discipline.** Discipline is frequently the backbone, the ultimate act of leadership. Handing the power of discipline to a subordinate is liable to prove more of a problem than a solution.

4. **The double-bossing menace.** A constant hazard in delegation is the possibility of double bossing, the situation where your subordinates find themselves responsible to two people.

When you do delegate a degree of supervisory control over others in the group, you can avoid conflict by—

► spelling out the exact nature of the responsibility you are delegating;

► defining clearly and publicly the limits of the authority you delegate;

► taking care of any complaints about overstepping boundaries promptly;

► making it clear to the subordinates involved to what extent they're to be led by your representative.

DELEGATION AS A DEVELOPER

Greater efficiency is only one of the possible benefits of delegation. There are four other important possibilities:

1. *You develop a subordinate's sense of responsibility.*
2. *You get him used to the "feel" of leadership.*
3. *You enlarge his general understanding.* For example, to show a subordinate the need for good customer relations, you might put him in charge of answering customer complaints.
4. *You increase his job satisfaction.* Many people thrive on varied assignments. Their interest in a job is increased with its responsibilities.

HOW TO KEEP CONTROL

As has been stated before, when you delegate responsibilities *you don't get rid of them.* You may hold your subordinate responsible; but, to the authority to whom you report, the responsibility is still yours.

Let's say a subordinate pulls a boner in the course of fulfilling a delegated responsibility. That's the case where the leader offers as an excuse to his superior: "Jones should have known better than to specify number-four stock for that order. We always use number three."

That's an excuse that doesn't excuse anything. It's up to the leader to retain sufficient control to avoid kickbacks. There are several possible ways to proceed:

Tell him the "rules." You avoid sour pay-offs by including with the delegation a list of "rules" by which the subordinate can handle situations your experience has shown are likely to occur. By making a standard specification and telling him to refer the exceptional cases to you, he himself will serve as a control.

Check the finished job. Another form of control is through an examination of the *results.* You simply examine the completed performance to see whether it's up to par.

Control by follow-up. In some cases, it may not be wise to wait until the performance is completed. This is particularly true where errors may be too expensive, or too hard to correct. You may want to check progress by inspecting, sampling, or spot-checking.

Progress reports. In some cases—because of a time element involved, location, etc.—the best plan may be to have your subordinate report on how he is making out.

Depending on the circumstances, such a report may be frequent or infrequent, written or oral, face-to-face or by telephone.

RESPONSIBILITY AND LEADER METHOD

There's a logical reason that explains *why* your leadership method does not influence your degree of responsibility. In almost all cases, you're given your leadership job—and its responsibility—without any directive as to what leadership methods to use. *These are your own choice.* In other words, a leader is delegated a responsibility, rather than a series of acts to perform. His carrying out of that responsibility is his basic job.

Regardless of the leadership method you use—whether autocratic, democratic, or free rein—the same responsibility still rests on your shoulders. And that remains true regardless of delegation or any other device you may use to lighten the work load.

As a matter of fact, it's precisely when the work load becomes tough that the effective leader tries to shed some of the details so that he is better able to *meet his over-all responsibilities.*

17 : *The Problem of Success*

If you could have your choice of problems, you'd probably choose the problem of success. You *might* be making a mistake.

BOLT FROM THE BLUE

To most of us, success seems to pose *no* problem. We think of the stock reaction to the complaints of the wealthy businessman: "I sure wouldn't mind having his troubles."

But past success is certainly no guarantee of an end to difficulties. In addition, under certain circumstances, success can actually prove a handicap. There's the commonly observed tendency, for example, to take things easy when one is riding the crest of the wave.

The result is, *one abandons the conduct that has won the success in favor of less demanding—and less efficient—methods.*

DEAD EAGLE

Fifty years ago, Eagle Coffee was one of the best-known, best-selling brands on the market, a household word from coast to coast. The leaders of that company had done a successful job, no question about it.

Eagle Coffee today? It's unknown, a thing of the past. Apparently the leadership that had been able to push the organization to the forefront in its field was unable to continue to function effectively in a success situation.

Certainly, the fate of Eagle Coffee is not unique. Hundreds of organizations—business or otherwise—have been born, have flourished, and gradually faded away. Why? What circumstances account for the sickening of a lusty, thriving organization? *What happens to its leadership?*

A number of scientific findings give us revealing answers to the question.

THE PSYCHOLOGY OF LETDOWN

A novel word-recognition experiment reported by David C. McClelland shows one of the significant ideas associated with the word *success.*

In the test, words were briefly flashed on a screen, but so dimly, in the beginning, that the subject could not possibly make it out. Nevertheless, he was asked to guess at the word. The level of illumination was gradually stepped up, and the subject was instructed to keep on guessing until he could actually identify the word. The theory is that before the word is consciously recognized, it is unconsciously perceived. Therefore, the guessed words indicate basic associations.

Here is one subject's list for the cue word, *success*:

either
become
woman
mother
empire
secure
success

The connection between "success" and "security" made by the subject explains a common attitude. And there's little question that the leader, basking in a feeling of security based on past successes, is less well poised for dynamic action than one tantalized by an unreached goal.

Some 2,000 years ago, the great lyric poet Horace put it this way: "Adversity has the effect of eliciting talents which in prosperous circumstances would have lain dormant."

Longfellow said, "It has done me good to be somewhat parched by the heat and drenched by the rain of life."

Our literature has repeatedly drawn the character who does great things in his years of poverty. Suddenly catapulted to the heights of fame and success, his accomplishment dwindles as his motivation is neutralized.

WHAT'S THE DEAL?

Belatedly, let me hasten to make a point.

Don't misinterpret the intent of this chapter. It's *not* an argument favoring failure. Its purpose is *not* to make success seem undesirable, *but to make it less fattening.* Success can slow a leader down—if he is unaware of the dangerous possibilities. Being aware of the hazards, however, you can take steps to offset them.

Psychologists have given us another set of findings which can help you make a better personal adjustment to success.

THE SUCCESS-FAILURE REACTION

Carefully controlled experiments with people have indicated:

1. Enjoying *success* makes most of us *raise* our sights.
2. Experiencing *failure* makes us *lower* our sights.

Under what *special* circumstances, then, does success tend to wet-blanket our efforts? Here are some of the possibilities:

► *When it's too easy.* Physicist Albert A. Michelson once said, "My greatest inspiration is a challenge to attempt the impossible." The success that can be had for the taking loses its appeal. We're less stimulated by it, less eager for it.

► *No new horizons.* An acquaintance, executive vice-president of a large retail enterprise, told me, "I'm in a hell of a spot. Here I am, at thirty-five, at the top of my profession." Whether he actually was at the top may have been debatable. But the fact remains that in his own eyes, success had left him without further incentives.

Many years before, a man named Alexander wept because he had no more worlds to conquer.

► *When the next step seems too big.* A really resounding success may put a leader in a position where his next step upward might call for a tremendous effort. In such a case, his slacking off of effort might be explained as an unconscious resistance to making an extreme effort, or to a fear that, making it, he might fail.

It's important to remember, however, that as a matter of fact, individuals respond *differently* to both success and failure.

WHAT'S YOUR PERSONAL REACTION?

Philemon wrote, "In this thing, one man is superior to other, that he is better able to bear prosperity or adversity."

What a Greek poet noted some 2,300 years ago, modern scientists have sought to verify. And their findings indicate that while, *in general,* success is a stimulant, and failure a depressant, to further effort, Philemon's observation that individual reactions vary is also true.

► The element of challenge, for some people, is *heightened by failure.*

► The element of challenge, for some people, is *lessened by failure.*

► The element of challenge, for some people, is *heightened by success.*

► The element of challenge, for some people, is *lessened by success.*

You will have to search your past experience to decide which—and to what extent—the four points above apply to you.

What the success-failure problem comes down to, essentially, is one of retaining in your work that stimulant, that goader to continued high-level effort, known as "challenge." Some of the things you do, and neglect to do, in the course of your leadership, determine the amount of challenge that surrounds you in your job.

YES MAN VS. CHALLENGE

In primitive groups, the leader was always subject to challenge. He retained his status just as long as he remained capable of besting his adversaries with fang, club, or cunning. As you might expect, mortality rates ran high among the self-satisfied and complacent leaders.

The situation remains fundamentally unchanged. That's why any factor that tends to narcotize leadership, lull it into feelings of oversecurity, is liable to be a handicap. That's why, for example, the yes man is insidious. He tends to fertilize the leader's self-satisfaction and inertia. He tends to minimize the element of challenge in the leader's environment.

Compare the quality of effort of executives A and B:

Mr. A: He has surrounded himself with a group of nice, pleasant fellows who admire him and veil the fact thinly. They applaud his every act and decision.

Mr. B: His lieutenants are a pretty hard-headed bunch. Their response to his ideas and decisions tend to be, "Let's see what's wrong with it."

Mr. A is actually handicapped. Without the stimulation and challenge which B gets from his assistants, he's *less* likely to maintain a high level of activity.

THEY FEED YOU TO TASTE

Keep in mind that it's *your* attitude that determines the attitude and responses of your subordinates. If you make it clear that you're after approval rather than honest opinion, you'll convert the most capable aides into rubber stamps.

If you're the kind of leader who dotes on the approval of your associates—and this category excludes practically nobody—you may want to consider this compromise. Have your yes man if you must. *But include in your staff at least one critic, one bumptious character who won't hesitate to needle you, or give you the business when the situation demands it.*

Here are two additional recommendations:

► *Raising your sights.* The benefit of challenge lies in its stimulation value. In physiological terms, it's an adrenalin activator. It supercharges you emotionally, provides the element that can make the difference between the lackadaisical and the inspired.

In more concrete terms, challenge generally gets you to do the thing that is an antidote for success slowdown: *it gets you to raise your sights.*

No matter how large or small the scope of your leadership, if you set yourself new and challenging goals, if you're continually seeking new worlds to conquer, success itself becomes not a drag but a horizon stretcher.

► *Dividing the laurels.* You can water down the satiating and self-glorifying effects of successes. It's merely a matter of passing along to your subordinates the praise and commendation for goals achieved.

HOW LINCOLN DID IT

Abraham Lincoln's sensitivity to the need to share success is revealed in a communication with one of his generals shortly after the Battle of Gettysburg.

Lincoln saw the possibility of ending the war by driving against Lee's retreating forces from the rear. He ordered General Meade to take this action by means of written instructions. A personal note was attached:

"The order I enclose is not of record. If you succeed, you need not publish the order. If you fail, publish it. Then, if you succeed, you will have all the credit of the movement. If not, I'll take the responsibility."

In thoughts and feelings like these lay Lincoln's greatness.

As far as is known, there is no case on record of group effort going sour because group members have been overburdened with the fruits of success. There are many cases on record where recognition by the leader of the efforts of his people has increased their loyalty and their appetite for more success.

18 : *Multipurpose Tool*

After her sisters had left for the ball, Cinderella sat down by the kitchen fire and cried. Immediately her fairy godmother appeared.

"Why are you crying, Cinderella?"

"Oh, I wish—I wish—"

"You wish to go to the ball?"

Cinderella nodded.

"Well, then, you shall. Run into the garden and fetch me the largest pumpkin you can find."

Cinderella did as she was bid.

Her godmother took the pumpkin and struck it with her wand. All at once, it became a splendid gilt coach, lined with rose-colored satin.

"How lovely!" cried Cinderella, clapping her hands happily.

THE MAGIC-WAND COMPLEX

Freudians aside, the Cinderella story certainly lays the cultural basis for much of our susceptibility to the magic-wand concept. Few of us forget the thrill of the godmother's magic. And with most of us remains the wish—at greater or lesser depth in our personalities—to have a magic wand of our own.

Of course, as we mature, the concept changes. The scout knife or other mechanical wonder-worker takes over for the youngster. For his older brother and his hobby-minded parent there is the five-way combination power tool.

THE WORLD OF IDEAS

As we mature, the tendency is for us to move from a physical world into a world of ideas. But we carry our susceptibility to the wonder-working gadget along with us. We look for the panacea, the intellectual gadget, the idea or approach that will solve all our problems.

THE ILLUSION SHATTERED?

Somehow, however, neither the mechanical gadget nor the universal problem-solver quite fulfills its promise. We learn that the screw-driver blade in the scout knife isn't as effective as a regular screw driver. And despite the implicit promise of its many blades, difficulties come up which elude *all* of them.

Similarly, the idea that should solve all problems is somehow reduced to ineffectiveness by the world of reality.

But this discouraging introduction can no longer disguise the fact that this chapter actually *does* offer for your consideration an intellectual gadget. It's a three-step approach that can be of material help in solving many of the problems you meet in carrying out your leadership functions.

The restraining note has been sounded at the outset to keep your expectations within reasonable bounds. The method *is* sound and has many uses. It also has very definite limitations.

MAGIC FORMULA COMING UP

Essentially, this idea is a problem-solving device. But here are some additional benefits it affords:

► *It provides a basic outline on which to build a problem-solving discussion or conference with associates.*

► *It can help you, and others working on a problem, to acquire more insight than usually results from most problem-solving attempts.*

► *It gives you a chance to get general agreement among a group as to what the specific problem actually is.*

► *Used in discussions with individual subordinates, it can give them an opportunity to approach their own problems with greater objectivity.*

POWERHOUSE IN A NUTSHELL

Essentially, the idea prescribes three steps for solving a problem. The three steps are:

Identification—pinning down the manifestations or symptoms of the problem.

Analysis—getting at the causes.

Solution—working out the action that will remove or minimize the causes.

HOW THE METHOD WORKS

Let's gauge the worth of this method by comparing it to another.

In the usual (ineffective) method, a works manager calls his supervisors together for a conference on absenteeism, saying, "Gentlemen, absenteeism is assuming serious proportions in our company. We've got to do something about it at once. I'd like to have your ideas."

One supervisor says, "I think we should have a stiff penalty. That will show the so-and-so's we mean busines."

The works manager asks for other suggestions.

Another supervisor: "Let's fire a couple of the worst offenders. The example is bound to have a good effect."

SOLUTIONS THAT SOLVE NOTHING

Perhaps the suggestions made by the foremen would have the beneficial results they intimate. But such off-the-cuff solutions usually create at least as many problems as they may solve. For example, studies generally give this kind of a picture as to reasons for absence:

Personal Illness—55 per cent
Personal Business—20 per cent
Family Illness—8 per cent
Accidents—5 per cent
Transportation—4 per cent
Miscellaneous—8 per cent

What would be the effect of a get-tough policy in a plant with this kind of absenteeism picture? It would probably bring to the job a certain number of sick or temporarily unfit individuals who would actually be better off at home. It would hinder a certain number from taking care of personal matters.

There's reason to believe that the resentment against this kind of pressure would have an adverse effect on employee morale and good will.

The basic objection to this method of problem-solving is that it overlooks entirely the *causes* of the problem. There are additional objections, which appear when the method is compared to the Identification, Analysis, Solution (I.A.S.) approach.

THE I.A.S. APPROACH

The works manager calls his group together and says, "Gentlemen, according to Mr. Smith of the Personnel Department, absenteeism has been getting out of hand in our company. Have you seen any evidence of this in your own department?"

I. THE IDENTIFICATION STEP

To help the conferees pin down the problem in specific terms, he says, "Let's get down to cases. Have any of you run into situations where you fell behind when a man was out, or where you had to put an added load on other people because of someone's absence?"

The information volunteered by the foremen at this point is calculated to—

► make them think of the problem in specific terms;

► give the conferees who are particularly aware of the problem the opportunity to tell their stories. Others, less aware of the problem, are then persuaded, by the evidence, that there *is* a problem.

► build an *over-all view* of the problem, as each person, by describing his contact with it, fits his particular piece of the jigsaw puzzle into place.

As this reconstruction of the problem from the ground up continues, the way is being prepared for a common view, an agreement that *first*, there is a problem, and *second*, what its dimensions are.

II. THE ANALYSIS STEP

Once the problem has been identified, you're ready for the analysis of the problem, the investigation of its causes.

The works manager now says, "I know you've talked to your absentees. What reasons do they give for staying out?"

The conferees' response to this question might include these items, along with the standard ones given in the previous list:

Poor transportation to the plant in bad weather.

Time lost on medical visits for minor ailments.

An individual not knowing he was scheduled to work that day.

III. THE SOLUTION STEP

In many cases, the identification and analysis steps are so revealing that they lead directly to obvious solutions. Take the three causes for absence above:

The company might contact the transportation people and see if special bad-weather schedules could be worked out.

The company might arrange, as many companies have, for minimal medical care either on the premises or at some convenient local medical office.

A foolproof method of work scheduling could minimize the "I didn't know I was supposed to work" problem.

FURTHER APPLICATIONS

Let's take another example, both to show another application of the I.A.S. approach and to illustrate how the application is partly influenced by the leadership method being used.

Joe Smith, sales manager, is faced by a problem of falling sales and a quarterly quota missed by a mile. Smith, who operates on democratic lines, gets his entire selling force together to discuss the failure. If he operated on an autocratic basis, he'd go through the procedure by himself, or with top assistants. If he led his group by the free-rein method, he'd ask each group member to go through the procedure individually.

I. IDENTIFICATION

Smith, to keep the discussion on a practical, realistic level, stays away from abstractions and generalities. He *doesn't* say, for example, "Gentlemen, we're not doing so good. What are we going to do about it?"

Instead, he talks in these terms:

Goal set: $1,000,000

Goal achieved: $600,000

Extent of failure: $400,000

II. ANALYSIS

Smith then asks his people to suggest reasons for the failure. Under the appropriate heading, the list looks something like this:

Causes of failure

"Goal too high."

"Salesmen sick."

"Poor communications." (One salesman wasn't given stock inventory situation he'd asked for, thereby losing a sale.)

At this point, Smith feels the causes given are too general, not hard-hitting enough. He asks, "Let's get down to individual cases. Did we *all* fail?" These points then emerge:

"Old-timers by and large made their individual quotas."

"New salesmen mostly didn't click."

When a checkup of figures verifies the fact, Smith then asks the new salesmen what their difficulties were. He gets this list:

"Too many 'cold' calls." (Also described as not enough co-operation from the home office.)

"Didn't know how to answer prospect's questions about the product."

"Competition tough." (Salesmen not well briefed on prospects' objections based on competitors' claims.)

III. SOLUTION

Smith completes the list of causes of failure, then goes over them one by one. For each, he asks, "What about this?"

For the first item, "Goal too high," the salesmen agreed that the sales goal was *not* too high.

Second: "Salesmen sick." Where men were put out of action by sickness, it was suggested that a colleague close the deals where delay might otherwise kill the sale.

Third: "Poor communications." It was decided to set up a new system, where each salesman would be assigned a personal contact in the home office.

And so on, down the list. There was general agreement on one major point which grew out of the poor records of new men. More training should be given before putting newcomers into the field.

THE INSIGHT FACTOR

Here's how an associate of mine used the I.A.S. approach to solve a problem arising from the unsatisfactory work of a newly hired subordinate.

The quality of the new man's performance was below standard. My colleague understood the essential difficulty: the new man had failed to fit into the work group. The tensions, and resultant emotional obstacles, were strong enough to reduce the man to ineffectuality.

It would have been simple enough for the employee to have been *told* what the trouble was. It is highly doubtful, however, whether he could then have gone on to do anything about it.

I. IDENTIFICATION

This is how my associate proceeded. He sat down with the employee and started a discussion about the man's work. The employee readily admitted that he was dissatisfied with the way things were going. He "guessed he wasn't catching on." However, when his superior pointed out that he certainly seemed to understand the procedures involved in his work, he agreed that "something was holding him back."

"What kind of things?"

After some thought he offered the following:

► He felt his fellow workers were giving him the cold shoulder in social exchanges. He wasn't included in their lunch circle, and so on.

► Whenever it was necessary for him to consult with anyone, he detected an unwillingness on their part to cooperate.

► He felt the man that had been assigned to break him in on his job had been unfriendly and unwilling to teach him the ropes.

Remember that up to this point *there had been little discussion of the man's work* as such. If a solution had been proposed which had been addressed entirely to the quality of the work—which on the surface seemed to be the central problem—the basic causes which the man was identifying *for himself* would most likely never have been touched on. And it scarcely seems likely that the emotional obstacle could have been dislodged.

II. ANALYSIS

My associate then asked what possible reasons or causes there were for this kind of behavior on the part of the work group. The employee immediately admitted that the fault was probably his own.

► He didn't mix readily with people.

► His first impression had been that there was some resentment against his getting that job rather than its being given to an old-time employee as a promotion.

► He felt his youth (he was five years younger than the average for the group) was a handicap.

III. SOLUTION

They went through the list of possible causes of the problem, eventually discarding all but the first. The employee then agreed that probably the best thing he could do to improve the situation was to make a positive effort to become integrated into the group. It was understood that his efforts would be made with the guidance and limited help of his superior.

IMPORTANCE OF THE I. AND A.

This example is particularly important because it demonstrates the opportunity offered by the two preliminaries to the solution step to gain an understanding, an insight into the problem.

Next time you have a problem of any kind, consider using the I.A.S. method in dealing with it. Unlike the one tool that gains in usefulness by adding gimmicks, until it resembles a porcupine, this approach is simple. But don't be misled by its simplicity. The uses to which it can be put are limited not by the elements it contains but by your ingenuity.

YOUR GOALS

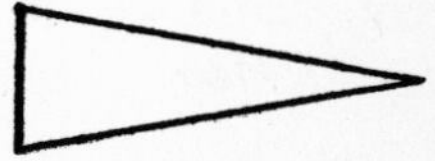

19 : *Setting Their Sights*

The annual Knights of Columbus ten-mile race at Quincy, Massachusetts, got off to an excellent start. The leading runners had already reached the first turn.

"Hey, that's the wrong way!" shouted two boys, standing at the corner.

Uncertain where they were going, the hard-pressed runners grasped at the youngsters' directions. But the "right way" found the entire field of forty athletes piled up in a dead-end street. Exasperated officials decided to call the race off till the following week.

GOAL?

Doubt as to where the goal is, or how to reach it, inevitably leads to confusion and aimless effort. It's true both of individuals and groups: there's the new housemaid who stands nonplused in the room she's been told to "clean up" because she doesn't know what the lady of the house actually has in mind. There's the gang of laborers, digging up a field in half-hearted fashion. They've been told to "start digging here and work toward the road." They haven't been told the objective—to locate a pipe line for which the blueprints have been lost.

The way you go about setting up objectives for your people has a profound effect on attitude and motivation. In one case, a goal can be made desirable, challenging, with the result that the group will drive itself to extreme limits to attain it. In another case, the leader's inability to make goals clear or attractive results in group apathy and disinterest.

The goals of a group may *seem* clear and uncomplicated. To the head of a retail sales department, for example, the means and ends of serving retail trade may appear fairly standard. But frequently in the very areas where group objectives seem routine there is most to be gained by re-examination of goal-setting practices. The element of freshness, of a changed perspective toward objectives can make the difference between a salesclerk yawning in a customer's face or yearning to make a sale.

GOAL!

As a nation, we're goal-minded. That's demonstrated by our emotional explosions at the sight of a player toting a football across the final white line of a sports field. It explains our feelings of admiration and respect for achievement—for people who have "arrived." Often it explains the pressure we put on ourselves to "get somewhere."

But being goal-minded can be a handicap. It's a handicap—

► *when the goal is illusory.* The social goal, to keep up with the Joneses, for example, tends to remain beyond reach. When we've caught up with Ed Jones next door, there's Tom Jones on the next street, whose car is in the next higher-price bracket. So-called "practical" goals can be of the same unreachable kind. The leader who sets an impossible goal for his group—"Next month we've got to triple our output"—will eventually find he's presented not a challenge, but an ultimate frustration.

► *when we lose more than we gain by reaching the goal.* The coach whose team wins a match "legally" but in unsportsmanlike fashion may at some later date wonder what it was he won after all. The supervisor who sets up a new standard of departmental conduct requiring that everybody "stick to his job, no moving around, no talking" may one day awaken to the fact that he's chilled off a good deal of the warmth in his work atmosphere. The Bible has something to say on this point, starting with the phrase, "For what is a man profited . . . ?"

► *when the goal is "wrong."* The leader may set the goal too high, too low, or in the wrong direction. The parent who fails to stimulate his children to develop their full capabilities is as much a failure as the one who puts the spurs to a potentially excellent mechanic with the injunction that he become a doctor. The company president who demands of his subordinates only that "they do as they're told" is thwarting their personal growth and stunting their ambitions and potential achievement—*as well as his own.*

YOUR GOAL-SETTING FUNCTION

Your ability to set goals for your group, and for individuals within your group, plays a major part in accomplishment. Generally, goals can be said to be of two kinds:

Short-range goals. You cover these, for example, under the heading of "job instructions." They're the objectives of your group's immediate activity.

Long-range goals. These can be either (a) the cumulative result of the day-to-day short-range goals—a year's quota achieved as a result of the day-to-day effort, or (b) they can be something separate and apart, as the degree of work satisfaction that an employee gets out of doing his job.

SHORT-RANGE GOALS

Sports—basketball, football, archery—provide the simplest and most graphic examples of goals. We can learn a good deal about the process of goal-setting from these popular activities.

1. **Make goals specific.** "Smith, it's important that your work be finished by the end of the week." If Smith and his boss agree on what's included in the phrase "your work," Smith may know what his boss is talking about. But most jobs consist of multiple assignments, many of them running concurrently. It's only when you tell Smith, "Please see to it that the Acme and National reports are finished up by Friday morning," that his goal becomes as clear as the finish line in a foot race.

Here are some additional goal-setting tips:

2. **Use numbers, where possible.** In giving out assignments, in issuing job instructions, it's often possible to state goals in numerical terms. Take advantage of this possibility. Consider the effectiveness of the device in instances like these:

► Progress report. Instead of, "Report back every once in a while," try "Report back at 9:30, 11, and 12."

► Time limits. Instead of, "Try to finish this job in short order," use, "This job should take two hours," or "until 4:00 to finish."

► Performance levels. (a) Quantity (to a new typist, for example). Not, "We expect a reasonable amount of work," but, "A reasonable aim is twenty letters a day." (b) Quality. Not, "All letters must be neat," but, "More than one erasure means we can't send out the letter."

Watch out for the slight chance of backfiring, however. When dealing with a literal-minded subordinate, here's what may happen: "Let's shoot at getting out one hundred pieces today," says the shipping-room head. The shipping clerk does ninety-five, and another five on overtime. "I didn't expect you to work overtime," complains his superior. "But you told me to do one hundred pieces," is the comeback. When you're dealing with this type of individual, state the goal as a range within which he's to work: "Between ninety and one hundred will be O.K."

3. **Provide specific tests or samples.** An ingenious mother, instructing her novice daughter on the art of cooking a turkey, gave the girl a piece of brown paper and the instruction, "When it turns this color, it's done."

You may be able to adapt some of these phrases that add clarity to goals:

"Stay with it until you get the cost down to two dollars."

"Let me know when the ratio hits 0:50."

"When the customer-load hits five hundred, we'll be ready for our next step."

LONG-RANGE GOALS

Long-range goals require a somewhat different approach from your efforts in the short-range area. To some extent, the time factor itself makes the basic difference. Long-range goals are subject to such hazards as—

► fatigue. We tend to get tired in the course of the long hauls. That shows up subjectively as the kind of doubt expressed by "Is it really worth while?"

► forgetting. Our memory tends to lose its grip on objectives, along with what we had for dinner last week, and "What was it I was supposed to do next Saturday night?"

Of course, a psychologist would hasten to point out that such memory loss is probably not unintentional. But unconscious or not, the result of the memory loss is the same: we lose sight of the goals we started out to reach.

► interference. Circumstances may alter the practicality of a goal. Let's say you're the publisher of a quality magazine. You have dedicated yourself and your group to maintaining high literary standards, don't want your pages cluttered up by anything as mundane as advertising.

Eventually, rising costs make it necessary for you to seek additional revenue. But to get decent advertising rates, you may have to increase circulation. And to increase circulation, you may have to look for a broader readership, which may mean a compromise with your standards of literary quality.

STAYING ON TARGET

It's uniquely your job, as a leader, to offset these and any other factors which tend to prevent group achievement of long-range objectives:

To counter *fatigue,* apathy, or loss of drive, you have to supply encouragement and stimulation.

As an antidote to *forgetting,* you have to keep objectives in view by (a) reminder: "That new method of assembly is fine, Jim, but don't forget, we're still aiming for a method to take the handwork out of that operation altogether"; (b) stressing its necessity: "It's important to all of us that the friendly and harmonious atmosphere in this group continues. It's at least as important as any other single thing we may accomplish."

The problem of *interference* becomes more meaningful—and your view of it more realistic—when you regard it as a *change* factor. Change of long-range goals is a symptom of growth. In some cases, they become obsolete because they are achieved. In others, they become less desirable compared to other needs.

Your alertness to the developments that bear on long-range aims will help make the adjustments—altering the goal and letting your group know about the change.

SOME POSSIBLE LONG-RANGE GOALS

If you're the publisher mentioned in the previous paragraphs, your long-range goal—and that of your editorial group—was to build a high-quality literary magazine.

Leaders who are in what are sometimes described as "creative fields"—research, publishing, teaching, for instance—tend to have long-range goals easy to describe. The head of a research department which is out to devise a better mousetrap can tell you his long-range goal in so many words.

But how about the business executive? Can the typical leader in the world of business set *any* long-range goals aside from production quotas, objectives other than improvements in operating efficiency—"doing things better . . . faster . . . at a lower cost"?

The answer is in the affirmative. Here are a few possibilities:

► *Increase in the feeling of unity and harmony within the group.* Since this is a matter of degree, it's a continuing goal. You help it along negatively by eliminating or minimizing frictions between individuals, by discouraging the formation of hostile cliques. On the positive side are your efforts to promote friendships and friendliness among your people.

► *Growth of the group.* The maturing of your group, its ability to act and react intelligently and with responsibility, is a function of your long-range goal setting.

It's important to recognize the comparative effectiveness of the three basic leadership methods in this regard. Group growth may be attained fairly easily by use of *democratic* methods and processes. But neither *autocratic* nor *free-rein* leadership is equally effective.

The explanation for the advantage of the democratic approach lies in group recognition of its own responsibilities. Since the group—*as a group*—participates in setting policy and lines of action, the results and consequences are always considered. It's this characteristic—action with an eye to consequences—that is typical of mature action.

There's no parallel in autocratic groups. Typically, activity is suggested by the leader. There can be little growth where there is no chance to break this rigid pattern. In the free-rein group, the growth of the group is largely a matter of growth of individuals.

► *Growth of the individual.* The leader can set up the goal of personal betterment for his people. You've undoubtedly seen examples of executives who do this. They're the ones who develop a reputation for doing an incubation job on a company's "geniuses."

Behind such a reputation you'll generally find a man who helps his subordinates along the path of self-development. He helps them spot their weak points, suggests courses of training that may eliminate them.

But the process of helping individuals grow in ability and self-confidence *varies with the different leadership methods.* Note the contrasts:

Autocratic method. Fred Greene, the autocratic leader of a sales organization, is interested in advancing several of his promising young men. He gives them assignments which *both test and train.* He encourages them to dig into their work, applauds when they make the sparks fly.

Under this treatment, they gain a more intimate knowledge of the work, pick up the fine points of selling and handling salesmen. But it should not be overlooked that essentially, Fred Greene is developing a number of little Fred Greenes. *He's making his assistants over in his own image.*

Desirable? It all depends. But before deciding whether this approach is the one to adopt, consider other possibilities:

Democratic method. Tom White, the democratic leader of a production organization, adopts a different course in developing the personal goals of his people. Some of his actions are the same as Fred Greene's: he gives his subordinates encouragement, for example, in their self-advancement efforts; he makes available to them the benefit of his experience in helping map out the course that will best strengthen weak points and build needed abilities.

He gives them frequent opportunity to develop their own ideas and approaches to problems. He gives them responsibilities, and enough authority to carry out the responsibilities on their own. The basic difference between him and Fred Greene is that he seeks to have his people develop *along lines best suited to their own personalities.*

Free-rein method. Henry Black, the free-rein leader of a research project, also wants his people to advance in their personal goals. To help them toward this end, he provides three things: (a) encouragement, the so-called "inspirational" motivation; (b) contacts with stimulating or challenging people and developments—this can mean anything from sending along reports of advances and development in the field to arranging for a trip abroad for the purpose of studying methods and progress of others in the field; (c) he tries to build an attitude of goal-mindedness.

The man who is being led by free-rein methods, more so than any other, must himself feel the worth-whileness of his work objectives. Where this is lacking, there's a strong tendency either to get lost in details of the work or to lose direction in basic activity. This is true because he largely lacks the partial sense of direction which people who work along with others get from the presence and activity of colleagues.

The individual whose growth is "administered" by the free-rein approach tends to be original, resourceful, and capable of carrying a large load of personal responsibility.

"FAST OR GOOD?"

Many a shop supervisor has been jolted by the employee who says, to a request that a rush job be done carefully, "I can do it fast or I can do it good. How do you want it?"

It's a fact that sometimes job objectives do—or seem to—conflict. To the conflicts between "fast and good," the leader has to work out practical answers. The answer may be, "Do the job as well as you can, and have it finished by three o'clock." Or it may be, "Tom, I know you're good enough at your job to do the job well up to standard *and* have it completed by three!" The person you're dealing with, the circumstances themselves, dictate your course of action.

CAN GOALS CONFLICT?

The conflict that poses a more difficult problem is the one that sometimes appears between short-range and long-range goals: you find yourself forced to trample on some cherished privilege which represents a part of your basic long-range aim, for the sake of immediate needs. You have to put individuals under pressure to achieve a short-range goal. It may ruffle tempers, cause frictions, but the end, you feel, justifies the means.

Here, too, your answer is necessarily a matter of striking a balance, of evaluating pros and cons, and making a decision. But—the real importance of goal conflict lies in another direction:

Behind the conflict is the vital fact that there is an *interdependence* between your short- and long-range objectives. The occasional conflicts are merely the exceptions that point up the logical need *for both sets of goals to be consistent.*

CAN METHODS CONFLICT?

This point has implications for your leadership method. ". . . People cannot be trained for democracy by autocratic methods," says Kurt Lewin in *Resolving Social Conflicts.* Lewin's statement can be interpreted to mean that you cannot hope to achieve long-range goals which are essentially democratic by using autocratic methods in setting short-range goals, and vice-versa.

You can achieve this consistency between ends and means by seeking the answers to these questions:

1. *What are my group's major short-range goals?*
2. *What leadership method is best suited to achieve these objectives?*
3. *What are the group's major long-range goals?*
4. *What leadership method is best suited to achieve these objectives?*

If the answer to questions 2 and 4 aren't the same, re-examine your statement of goals, and the thinking that has led to selection of the leadership methods.

THE SLIGHT EDGE

A baseball game won by 1–0 goes as solidly into the victory column as a 12–1 score.

Moral? Victory is usually not the result of tremendous superiority. One run does it as surely as eleven. The difference between success and failure in meeting a tough schedule, for example, may depend on an extra ounce of effort, a shade more teamwork.

The idea of the "slight edge" is an argument in favor of aiming toward slight improvements, slight advancements of the goal. You have a better chance to achieve the goal. And that achievement then becomes a springboard for the next forward move.

Selling this idea to your subordinates can help them take a more realistic approach to their work. Those who are light on self-confidence will take more readily to the less frightening challenge.

The leader who asks his people to cut waste in half is apt to leave discouragement or loud horselaughs in his wake. But the leader who says, "Next month let's cut our waste percentage by 5 per cent" is presenting a goal that's possible on its face. And he's on solid ground when the following month he says, "We cut waste down 5 per cent last month. Let's see if we can't repeat this month."

SKY'S THE LIMIT

The "slight-edge" concept is significant in setting short-range goals. *But the same device will weaken the motivations of your group if carried over into long-range objectives.*

As a matter of fact, the most effective leader has always been the man who set "impossible" long-range goals. Even for the most timid, the buffer of time serves to eliminate the fear of imminent failure. And to the average subordinate, nothing is more inspiring than the leader who puts into words the group's ultimate hopes of security and achievement. As were the people of the Bible, people today are also eager to follow the man who holds up the vision of "a promised land."

20 : *Keeping Leadership Up-to-date*

"He that will not apply new remedies must expect new evils," said Bacon.

Whether or not Sir Francis specifically had leadership in mind, there's little doubt that to avoid the evils of obsolescence, your methods require continual readjustment. However, adjusting leadership is not a matter of taking action when the slip begins showing.

No, the constant policing of your leadership methods is more than a holding action. True, today's problems outgrow yesterday's solutions. But there is another and more challenging reason for change. *Your leadership skill has the capacity to grow*. By maintaining a flexible approach, by periodic checks of the aptness of present methods, you can make the changes that are the outward signs of increase in leadership stature.

There is no one standard pattern of changing needs. You may go along for some time without visible evidence of changes taking place. Over a period of time, however, subtle but telltale evidences will begin to accumulate: your relationships start to misfire; working arrangements you have set up within the group don't click as well as they did; you seem to be working in an atmosphere of increasing pressure.

MEETING CHANGE WITH CHANGE

Frequently, it is possible to provide positive and pinpointed tests for changing leadership requirements. And you can make these tests in several different areas.

A series of factors hold the clues. These can help you determine whether current methods are still valid, or whether they've passed over into the class of the crystal set and the celluloid collar.

Here, in the form of a streamlined check list, are the things which can help you decide whether or not it's time for a change.

I. DEALINGS WITH INDIVIDUALS

The kid who started green last year may be your hot shot today. The outlook of your key men of yesterday may have undergone radical changes. As you go through the questions below, keep individual subordinates in mind.

1. Anyone gone stale, whose interest and drive can be stepped up by increased responsibility, freer rein?
2. Anyone whose efforts are flagging because of lack of direction and the need for *more* guidance?
3. Have any newcomers caught on to their jobs well enough to warrant—
   (a) an *easing* of some of your control?
   (b) additional functions which would represent a step upward or forward?
4. If your use of the democratic method has been unsuccessful with certain individuals, is it possible you could improve results by—
   (a) an explanation of what is expected of them in group matters?
   (b) encouragement to *participate* more actively—in conferences, for example?
   (c) assignments which would make it difficult for them to remain passive in group activities—such as responsibility for making reports, and so on?
5. If you have recently noticed that some of your old-timers are beginning to founder, is it possibly because—

(a) advancing age has made them less able to carry as large a responsibility as before?
(b) you have unconsciously given them an overload, with insufficient help or control on your part?

6. If you have a case of the "overdependent subordinate" on your hands, the man who is always "checking back," is it because—
(a) you've mistakenly given too free a rein to someone who needs guidance?
(b) you're using the autocratic method, not giving the man enough information, and at the same time insisting that the "job be done your way"?
(c) you have failed to provide or to tell him about other sources besides yourself from which he can get information?

7. If you've been stung by a subordinate acting on his own initiative and making decisions you disagree with—
(a) is it because you are *inadvisedly* using the free-rein method?
(b) you've delegated responsibilities that actually you should retain?
(c) you've failed to make clear the limits in which he is free to act on his own?

8. The autocratic method, maintained with an individual showing decided personal growth, tends to block his further development. Does this fact explain any case of a subordinate who has recently—
(a) seemed to resent your authority?
(b) shown signs of losing interest in his work?
(c) become "restless" on the job?

FURTHER ANALYSIS

Along the lines indicated by the questions above, isolate cases where your relations with individuals have soured, or have failed to develop as well as you feel they should. Then try to answer these two questions:

► What has been the basic nature of the leader-subordinate relationship—

(a) autocratic?
(b) democratic?
(c) free rein?

► What change or modification of method might improve the relationship? ____ ____ ____ ____ ____ ____ ____

____ ____ ____ ____ ____ ____ ____ ____ ____ ____

II. DEALINGS WITH THE GROUP

Changes in a group come about for several reasons: there's the cumulative effect of all the changes to which the *individual* is prone—aging and maturity, growth of experience, and so on. In addition, people leave to get married or for better jobs. Others are promoted or transferred. The final result may be a numerical increase or decrease. And the goals of the group may have changed, either increased or decreased in scope.

These changes, or similar ones, may raise the following questions for you:

1. Has a change in group size outmoded previous methods of communication, such as:
   (a) informal meetings or get-togethers?
   (b) your habitual means of establishing face-to-face contact?
   (c) your method of "passing the word around" in lieu of written announcements, or vice versa?
2. Has a change in the type of people you have in your group made advisable readjustments in leadership method?
   (a) If a higher percentage of your people are now skilled workers, is the group as a whole more capable of getting by on its own, via the free-rein approach?

(b) On the other hand, if the increase has been in the direction of lowering the level of experience, is more autocratic leadership desirable?
(c) If the background of your people—either educational or otherwise—is such as to make them more susceptible to it, would an increase in democratic techniques be suitable?

3. Has the average age of your group changed sufficiently—
   (a) by addition of older people, or the ordinary march of time—to suggest a greater ability to shoulder responsibility, participate more in group decisions?
   (b) through the addition of numbers of youngsters—so as to bring about a greater need for autocratic methods?
4. Has your group increased its percentage of untrained help, requiring stronger control and more guidance?
5. Have group goals changed—so that achieving them requires—
   (a) less group drive but more individual initiative (suggesting greater dependence on free-rein methods)?
   (b) less individual initiative but more integration of individual effort in harmonious group action (best achieved by democratic methods)?
   (c) less participatory activity on the part of the group, but greater goal-directed effort (best achieved through autocratic processes)?
6. If your group has been more or less recently formed—
   (a) has it come of age, thus meriting a shift from autocratic techniques to the democratic or free-rein approaches?
   (b) has an increasing ability of the group to work harmoniously together made it advisable to depend more heavily on democratic methods?
7. A general laxness can afflict a group with poor disciplinary atmosphere, attendance, excessive gripes and grievances.

If anything of this nature has come about recently, would it be advisable for you to use more autocratic methods—

(a) in enforcing rules and policies?

(b) in devoting more of your personal time to direct working contact with your people?

FURTHER ANALYSIS

Use the questions above as examples of the kind of problems that can outmode your leader-group relations. Try to put your finger on instances where your relations with the group as a whole have been unsatisfactory: failure to get acceptance for your policies, resistance to new methods, and so on. Then look for answers to these questions:

What was the nature of the friction with the group? ____

Why, *basically*, did it come about? ____ ____ ____ ____ ____ ____ ____ ____ ____ ____ ____ ____ ____

What acts of leadership might have prevented or minimized the problem? ____ ____ ____ ____ ____ ____ ____ ____ ____ ____ ____ ____ ____ ____ ____ ____ ____

III. THE SITUATION FACTOR

Times change. The circumstances under which you and your group operate are affected by many outside events. They may take place at a world-wide or national scale, or in your own back yard.

New ideas, a new spirit, influence the attitudes and behavior of your people. Consider whether changes either in the circumstances or the atmosphere affecting you and your group suggest alterations in your leadership approach. Here are a few possibilities:

1. Has the physical work area of your group changed? If so—
   (a) should you be reconsidering your delegation arrangement—either more or fewer delegations, for example?
   (b) is it economical for you to supervise the work directly, and accordingly, might current autocratic methods be replaced by the self-policing techniques available in either the democratic or free-rein procedures—or vice versa?
2. Do increased demands on your own personal time make it desirable to train more of your people to the point where they can get along with less of your time?
3. Has an increase of competitive pressure on your organization made advisable a change of approach either—
   (a) along the lines of enlisting greater participation from your group by using more democratic techniques?
   (b) by a transmission to your group of this pressure through autocratic processes?
4. Uncertainties from the outside may penetrate into the world of the group. If so, would a shift of leadership along autocratic lines add a reassuring note?
5. Frequently, your leadership method must take into account specific outside situations, such as a tight labor market, for example. If such a situation is making your group restless, is increasing turnover rates, would an increase in democratic methods increase feelings of group unity, strengthen personal relationships, and thus heighten job satisfaction?
6. Has an increase in the difficulty of the work—sometimes a result of operational changes, like use of new materials or procedures—made less desirable a free-rein approach, increased the need for you to direct group activity along autocratic lines?
7. Intraorganizational pressures on your group may sometimes become a threat. A common example is the "battle of departments." Regardless of the merits of the "con-

flict," is it advisable for you to sit more firmly in the driver's seat, guide your group through the crisis?

8. For reasons unknown, group tempers may change. Are you using the best leadership method to cope with the current group mood?

FURTHER ANALYSIS

The questions above suggest a few of the ways in which the situation can affect what will or won't constitute effective leadership. If other circumstances are influencing your group's feelings or behavior, answers to the following questions may help you weigh possible leadership adjustments:

Essentially, what is the nature of a new pressure on the group?____ ____ ____ ____ ____ ____ ____ ____ ____
____ ____ ____ ____ ____ ____ ____ ____ ____ ____

What specific effects is it having on group performance or feelings? ____ ____ ____ ____ ____ ____ ____ ____
____ ____ ____ ____ ____ ____ ____ ____ ____ ____

IV. PERSONAL CONSIDERATIONS

You yourself are as prone to change as any of the elements in the leadership complex. Your viewpoint grows and matures. Your feeling about *problems* changes. Last year's problem, encountered this year, seems less critical, considerably easier to handle. Your feeling about *solutions* also changes. The kind of solution that may have seemed fine yesterday might seem immature, superficial, or merely inadvisable in the light of your current views.

Here are some specific points to check:

1. Do you find you're not getting enough emotional satisfaction out of your work? You might consider a change of approach if you could characterize yourself along any of these lines—

(a) the "lonely autocrat"?
(b) the "frustrated democrat"?
(c) the "out-of-contact free-rein leader"?

2. On becoming more familiar with your job, you may feel you can relax control. Does this call for greater use of democratic or free-rein methods?

3. It may be desirable for you to develop assistants. The people you choose as sub-leaders can be trained by the process of delegation. Does this call for a reconsideration of your delegation practices—
   (a) the individuals to whom you've delegated responsibilities?
   (b) reponsibilities delegated?
   (c) the degree of independence you permit them by your leadership method?

4. Have your personal goals shifted, so that the possibility of your advancement possibly makes advisable more self-regulation by the group (democratic approach)?

5. If you feel performance levels are unsatisfactory, is it possible that your group's response to a change in leadership methods might influence their—and your—performance?

6. If relations with specific individuals in your group are poor from *your* standpoint, are alterations in your leadership method indicated?

7. If the mood of your group leaves something to be desired, is it possible that a revised leadership approach might bring about worth-while changes, such as—
   (a) more obedience through more autocratic devices?
   (b) more participation through more democratic devices?
   (c) more initiative through more free-rein devices?

8. Have you gone stale? Is there a need for you to explore and experiment with leadership methods as a means of tapping unknown potentials—both for you yourself and for your subordinates?

FURTHER ANALYSIS

Are you happy in your job? (This is just one of the possible ways of saying, "Do you feel you're performing satisfactorily? "Are your superiors satisfied with your performance?")

If not, could a change in your relationships with subordinates affect the picture?

What changes would have to take place? ____ ____
____ ____ ____ ____ ____ ____ ____ ____ ____ ____

What leadership methods would be the best implementation for these changes? ____ ____ ____ ____ ____
____ ____ ____ ____ ____ ____ ____ ____ ____ ____

Could a change in your relations with your superior affect the picture?

What changes do you think might be advisable? ____
____ ____ ____ ____ ____ ____ ____ ____ ____ ____

What leadership methods that your superior might use—*and that you might get him to adopt*—do you think might bring about the desirable changes? ____ ____ ____ ____
____ ____ ____ ____ ____ ____ ____ ____ ____ ____

INDEX

Q

R

S

About the Author

Born in New York City, Mr. Uris went through the public school system and into the City College of New York, class of '34. His background in the field of leadership and human relationships, in which he specializes, was gained from personal experience. For five years he was a supervisor in a large plastics plant and for several years was owner and manager of a custom molding shop. During his career in management he became interested in studying the human-relations data being developed at such research centers as Harvard University, the University of Iowa, Columbia University, and the National Research Council.

His present work in the Human Relations Division of the Research Institute of America, which started in 1947, makes available to him the leadership experience—in both problems and solutions—of hundreds of organizations, thousands of executives in the business world.

Mr. Uris has an all-girl family—three daughters, Mary, Victoria, and Bettina, and his wife, Bette Turner Uris. This group provides a tough but realistic proving ground for many of his leadership—and followership—ideas.

In addition to three books—*Improved Foremanship*, *Working with People*, and *How to Be a Successful Leader*—he has written numerous magazine articles on human relations and management.